CW01594263

Internet Explorer 5.5 Outlook Express 5

QUICK FIX

Internet Explorer 5.5

Outlook Express 5

John Ralph

QUICK FIX

TEACH YOURSELF BOOKS

For UK orders: please contact Bookpoint Ltd, 78 Milton Park, Abingdon, Oxon OX14 4TD. Telephone: (44) 01235 400414, Fax: (44) 01235 400454. Lines are open 9.00 – 6.00, Monday to Saturday, with a 24-hour message answering service. E-mail: orders@bookpoint.co.uk

British Library Cataloguing in Publication Data
A catalogue record for this title is available from the British Library.

First published 2001 by Hodder Headline Plc, 338 Euston Road, London, NW1 3BH.

The 'Teach Yourself' name and logo are registered trade marks of Hodder & Stoughton Ltd. Computer hardware and software brand names mentioned in this book are protected by their respective trademarks and are acknowledged.

Copyright © 2001 John Ralph

All rights reserved. No part of this publication may be reproduced or transmitted in any form or by any means, electronic or mechanical, including photocopying, recording, or any information storage and retrieval system, without permission in writing from the publisher or under licence from the Copyright Licensing Agency Limited. Further details of such licences (for reprographic reproduction) may be obtained from the Copyright Licensing Agency Limited, of 90 Tottenham Court Road, London W1P 9HE.

Typeset by Elle and P.K.McBride, Southampton
Printed in Great Britain for Hodder & Stoughton Educational, a division of Hodder Headline Plc, 338 Euston Road, London NW1 3BH by Cox & Wyman, Reading, Berkshire.

Impression number	10 9 8 7 6 5 4 3 2 1
Year	2006 2005 2004 2003 2002 2001

Contents

INTERNET EXPLORER 5.5

Introduction

Set up an Internet connection

1. In the **Tools** menu click **Internet Options…**
2. Under the **Connections** tab, click **Setup…**
3. Follow the instructions given by the wizard.

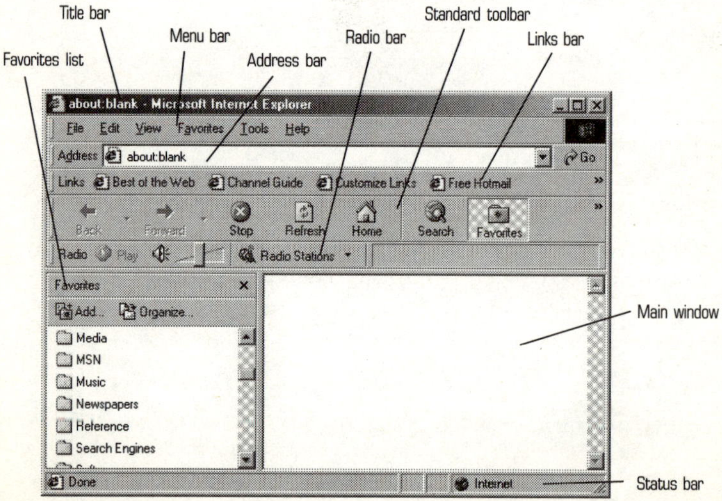

Open a web page

1. Left click in the **Address bar** and type the Internet address.
2. Click on **Go**.

Or

Press **Enter**.

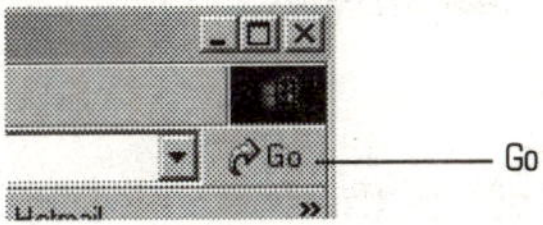

tip

Information for the connection settings can be obtained from your Internet Service Provider. Write it down somewhere safe in case you need it again.

Use the stop button

If a page you are trying to open is very slow to display:

1. Click 

.

Or

Press **Esc**.

> **tip**
>
> The blue progress bar in the status bar grows longer even when no data is being received. Do not rely on it for information on download progress.

Use the refresh button

To get the latest version of the page, or if you are informed that a Web page cannot be displayed:

1. Click .

Or

Press **F5**.

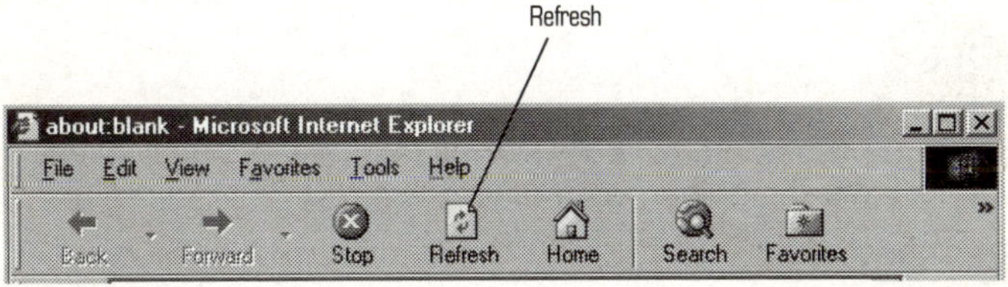

Speed up display

1. In the **Tools** menu click on **Internet Options…**

2. Under the **Advanced** tab scroll to the **Multimedia** icon.

3. Clear any or all of the **Show pictures**, **Play animations**, **Play videos**, or **Play sounds** check boxes.

tip

With the **Show pictures** or **Play videos** check boxes disabled a picture or animation on a Web page can still be displayed by right-clicking on its icon (×), and then clicking **Show pictures**.

Run a program

1. In the **Address bar**, type the program path and name – for example: C:\Windows\Freecell.exe

2. Click on the **Go** icon.

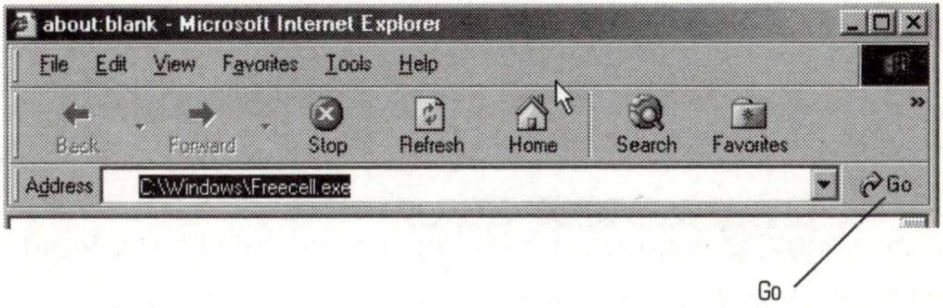

Link to visited sites with Forward/back buttons

To return to the previously viewed page, click .

To see a page you viewed before clicking **Back**, click .

To select from a list of the last few pages you visited, click the down arrow beside the **Back** or **Forward** buttons.

Drop down the list of visited sites

Link to your home page

To return to your starting page click the  button.

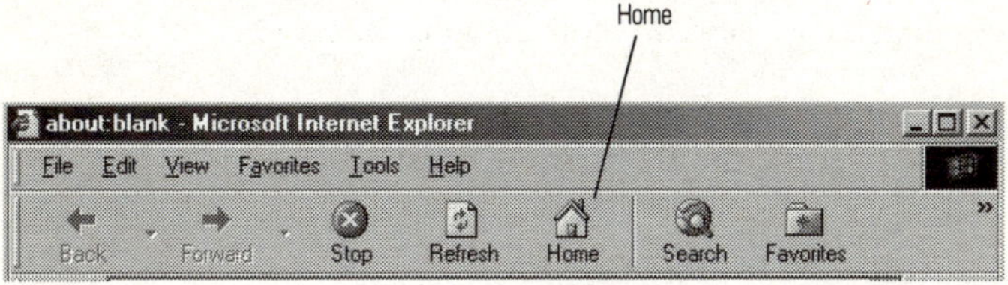

tip

See page 53 for further information.

Link to a memorized page

1. Click on the **Favorites** icon.
2. Select the required Web page from the list.

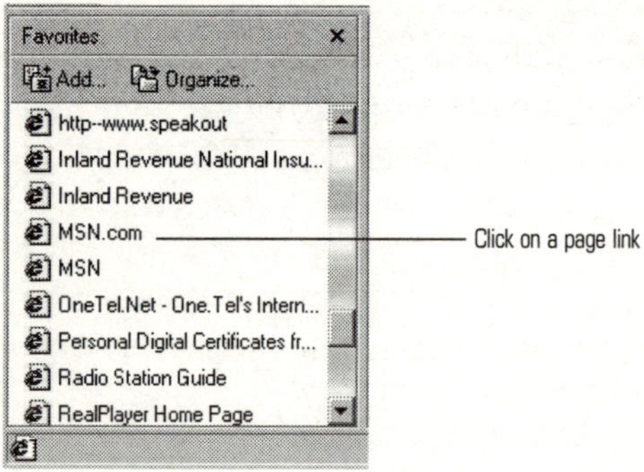

Use AutoComplete

1. In the **Address bar**, or a field on a Web page, or a box for a username or password, start typing the information.

2. If you have used a similar entry before, **AutoComplete** suggests matches as you type.

3. If a suggestion in the list matches what you want to enter in that field, click it, if not, continue typing.

tip

No AutoComplete information is accessible by Web sites. It is encrypted on your disk for privacy.

Delete individual AutoComplete entries

You can remove an item from the list of suggestions by clicking it and then pressing **Delete**.

tip

This works only when typing in Web forms and typing passwords.

Delete AutoComplete entries from the Address bar list

1. In the **Tools** menu click on **Internet Options...**

2. Under the **General** tab, in the **History** section, click on **Clear History**.

tip

This clears all items from your History folder. You cannot clear individual entries from the list of saved entries in the Address bar.

Adjust AutoComplete settings

1. In the **Tools** menu click on **Internet Options…**

2. Under the **Content** tab, in the **Personal information** section, click on **AutoComplete…**

3. Select the check boxes for the **AutoComplete** options you want to use.

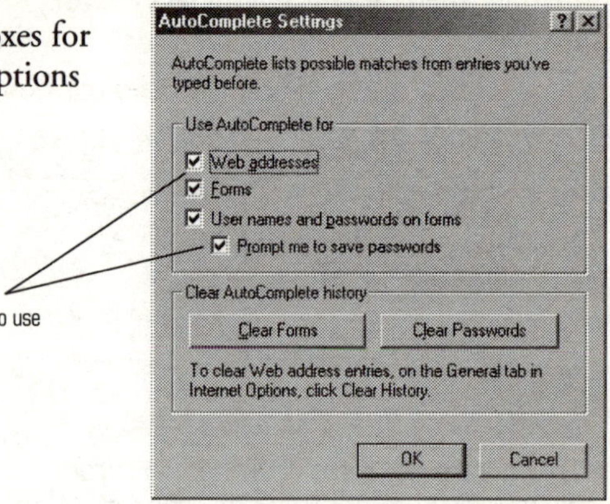

Tick those you want to use

tip

You can select/deselect AutoComplete for addresses, passwords and forms. AutoComplete History can also be cleared.

Searching

Find information on the Web

1. Click .
2. Type a word or phrase in the **Search** box.
3. Click on **Search**.

Or type **go**, **find**, or **?** in the Address bar, followed by a word or phrase and then press **ENTER**.

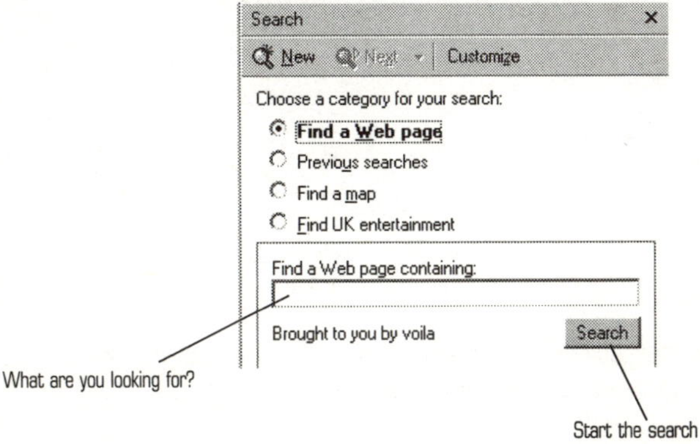

Find information on a Web page

In the **Edit** menu click **Find (on This Page)…**

Or

Hold down **CTRL** and press **F**.

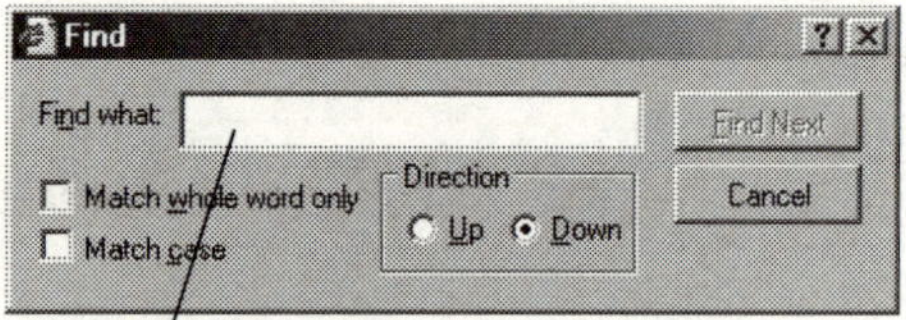

Enter the word(s) to find

Perform category searches

1. Click 

.

2. Choose a category.

3. Fill in the new prompts as required.

4. Type the information that you are looking for, and then click **Search**.

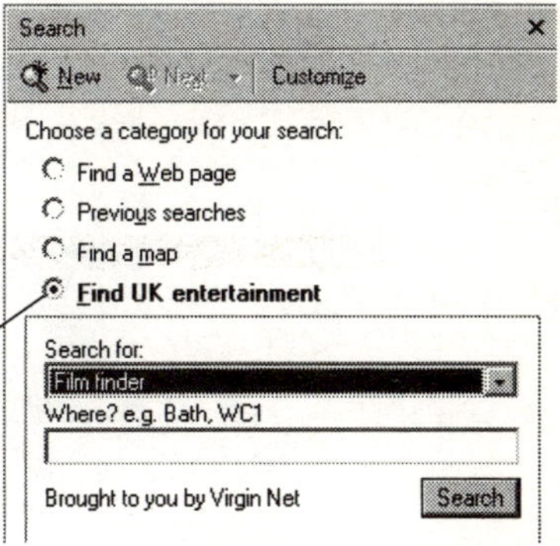

Choose a category

tip

The more information you type in each field, the better the results of the search.

Find related sites

1. In the **Tools** menu click **Show Related Links.**

2. Links to Web pages similar to the one you are currently viewing will be shown.

Click on Show Related Links

tip

You must be online to use this search facility.

Search from the address bar

You can view search results in several ways:

1. In the **Tools** menu in **Internet Explorer**, click on **Internet Options…**

2. Under the **Advanced** tab, in the **Search from the Address bar** section, select an option.

Select an option

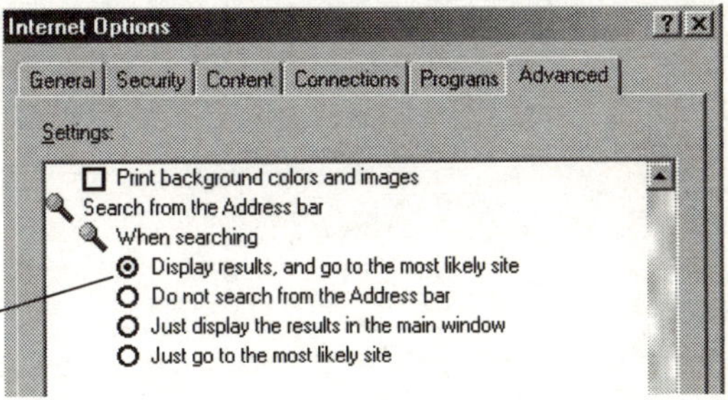

tip

Changing these options does not affect searches using **Search**.

Find recent pages

1. Click .

2. In the **History** bar that appears, click a week or day, click a folder and then click a page icon to display the Web page.

3. Click  again to hide the **History** bar.

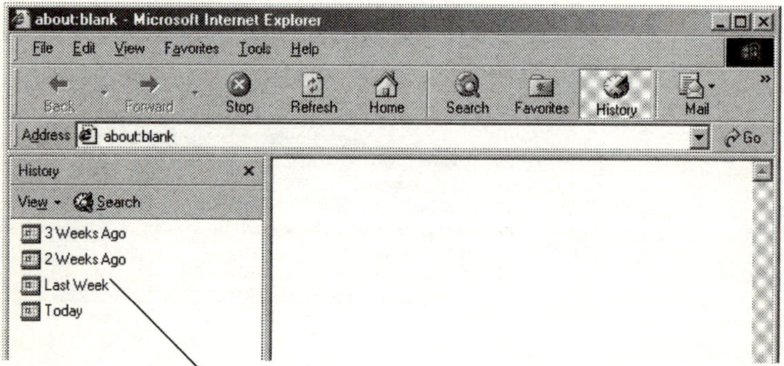

Open a folder and click on a link

tip

To sort or search the History bar, click the arrow next to the View icon at the top of the History bar.

Alter the History period

1. In the **Tools** menu click on **Internet Options…**

2. Click the **General** tab.

3. Under **History** change the number of days to track your pages.

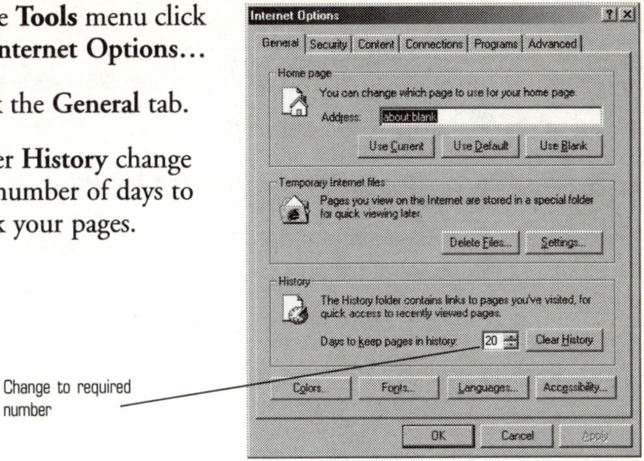

tip

The longer the specified period, the more disk space is used. To free space on your disk click on Clear History.

Favorites

Add a Web page to favorites

1. Go to the Web page you want to add.

2. In the **Favorites** menu, click on **Add to Favorites…**

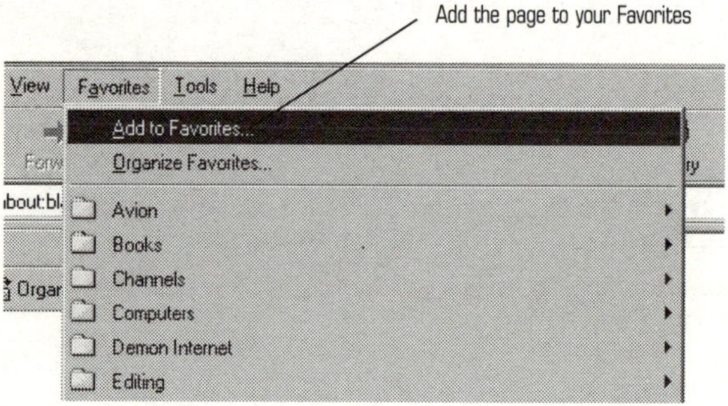

tip

You can give the page a new name in your Favorites list.

List your Favorite pages

1. Click .

2. Click the shortcut in the **Favorites** list to open the page.

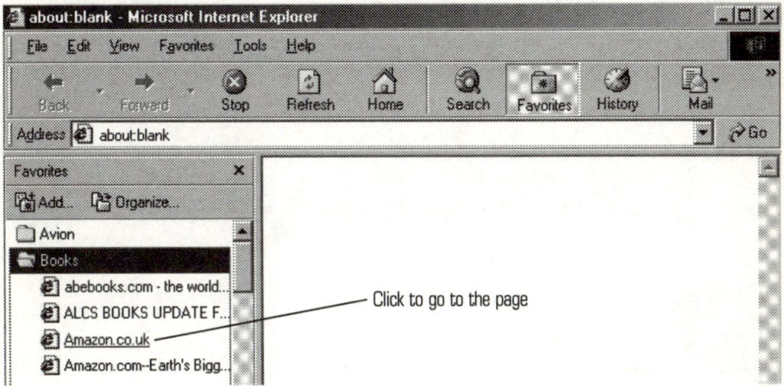

tip

If you visit some sites frequently you can add them to your Links bar (see page 28).

Organize favorites into folders

1. In the **Favorites** menu, click on **Organize Favorites…**

2. Click **Create Folder**, type a name for the new folder, and then press **ENTER**.

3. Drag the shortcuts (or folders) in the list to the appropriate folders.

Or

Use the **Move to folder** button.

tip

You can drag shortcuts in your list from folder to folder.

Change your Home Page

Your home page is the page that appears every time you open Internet Explorer.

1. In the **Tools** menu, click on **Internet Options…**

2. Under the **General** tab, in the **Home Page** section, select your choice.

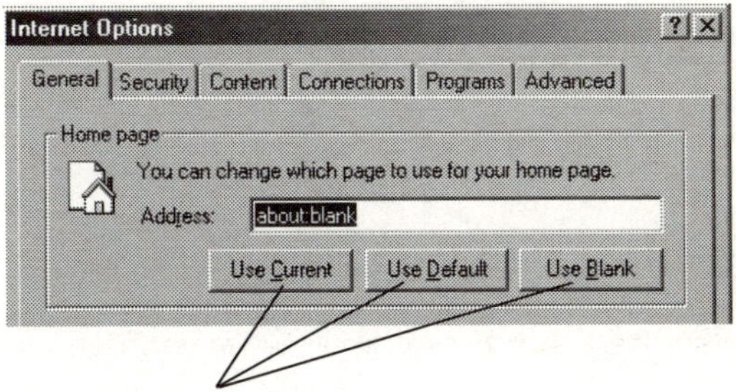

Click to select as your home page

tip

Click **Use Default** to restore your original home page.

Share favorites

To import or export favorites or bookmarks (Netscape's name for favourites):

1. In the **File** menu, click on **Import and Export...**

2. Follow the wizard's instructions.

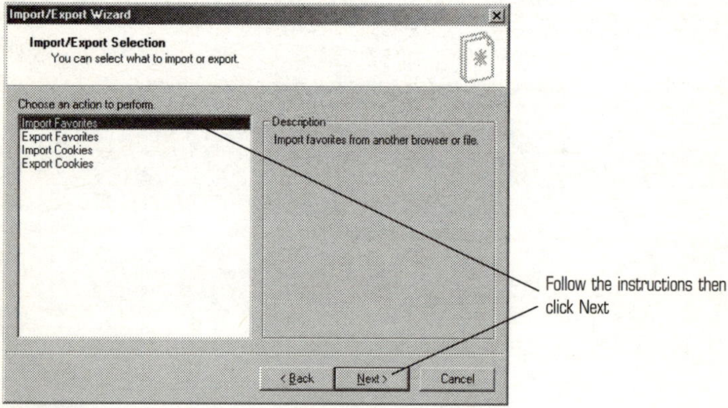

tip

Favorites are exported as a normal HTML file and can be easily shared via floppy disk or e-mail.

Show the Links bar

To show the Links bar:

1. Right-click on the toolbar.

2. Click on **Links**.

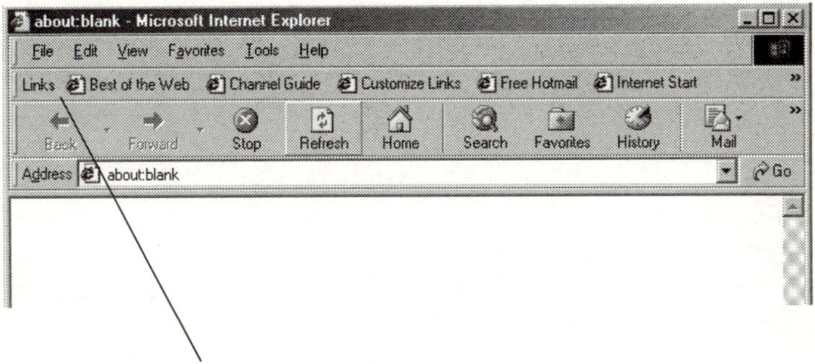

The Links bar

tip

Here you can add links to Web pages that you use frequently. To display the page click the link.

Add a page to your links bar

Drag the page icon from the Address bar to the Links bar.

Or

Drag a link from a Web page to the Links bar.

Or

Drag a link to the Links folder in your Favorites list.

tip

If the **Links** bar is not in view, in the **View** menu, point to the **Toolbars** icon, and click on **Links**.

Offline viewing

Make current page available offline

1. In the **Favorites** menu, click **Add to Favorites…**

2. Tick the **Make available offline** check box.

3. To detail how you want the page updated click on **Customize…** and follow the instructions on screen.

tip

Before going offline get the latest version of your pages. In the **Tools** menu click on **Synchronize…**

Make a favorite available offline

1. In the **Favorites** menu click **Organize Favorites…**
2. Click the page you want available offline.
3. Tick the **Make available offline** check box.
4. To detail how you want the page updated click **Properties**.

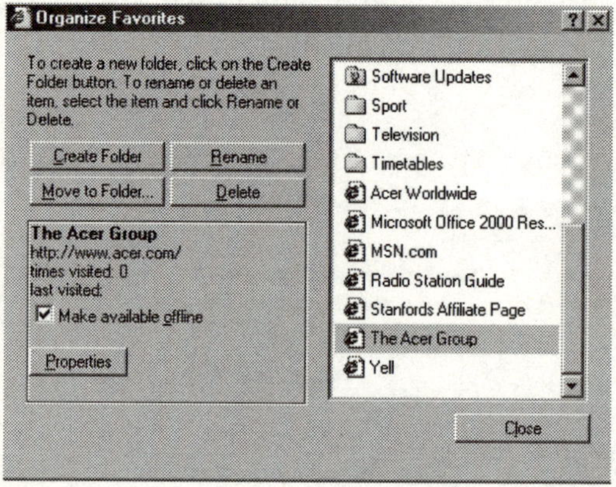

Save a Web page on your computer

1. In the **File** menu, click **Save As...**

2. Double-click the folder you want to save the page in.

3. In the **File name:** box, type a name for the page.

4. In the **Save as type:** box, select a file type:

   Web Page, complete (***.htm,*.html**) to save all the graphics, frames and style sheets needed to display this page. This option saves each file in its original format.

   Web Archive, single file (***.mht**) to save a snapshot of the current Web page.

   Web Page, HTML only (***.htm,*.html**) to save just the current HTML page. This option saves the information on the Web page, but not the graphics, sounds, or other files.

   Text File (***.txt**) to save just the current Web page text.

5. After selecting the format click **Save**.

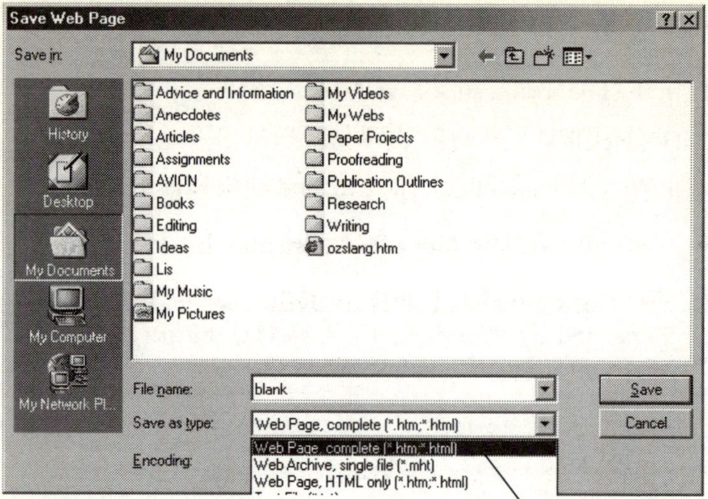

Save as a Web Page

tip

With **Web Page, complete (*.htm,*.html)** and **Web Archive, single file (*.mht)**, all the Web page can be viewed offline, without adding the page to your Favorites list and marking it for offline viewing.

Save pictures or text from a Web page

- Save a page or picture without opening it:

  Right-click the link for the item and click **Save Target As…**

- Copy information from a Web page into the clipboard:

  Select the information, click the **Edit** menu and click **Copy**.

- Create a desktop shortcut to the current page:

  Right-click in the page and click **Create Shortcut**.

- Use a Web page image as desktop wallpaper:

  Right-click the image, and click **Set as Wallpaper**.

- Send a Web page in an e-mail:

  In the **File** menu, point to **Send**, and then click **Page by E-mail…** or **Link by E-mail…**

View Web pages without being connected

After you mark your favourite pages for viewing offline:

1. Before disconnecting from the Internet, in the **Tools** menu click on **Synchronize...**

2. When ready, in the **File** menu click **Work Offline**.

3. In your **Favorites** list click the page to view.

tip

Having chosen to work offline, Internet Explorer will start in Offline mode until you click **Work Offline** again to clear the check mark.

Printing

Print a whole Web page

Click on .

Or

Hold down **CTRL** and press **P**.

Or

In the **File** menu select **Print...**

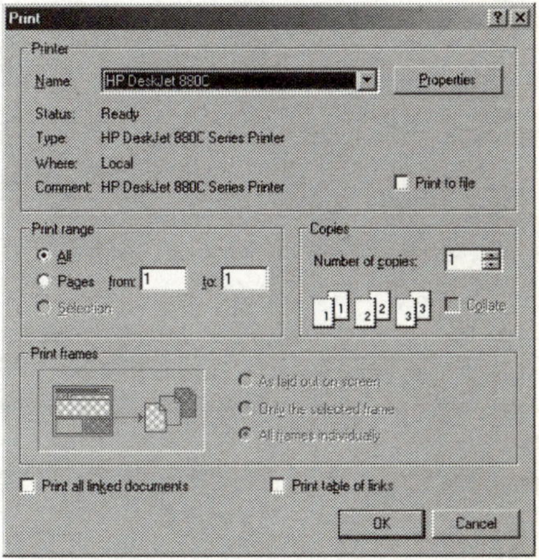

Print part of a Web page

To print a frame or an item in a Web page:

1. Right-click the frame or item.
2. Click **Print…** or **Print Target**.

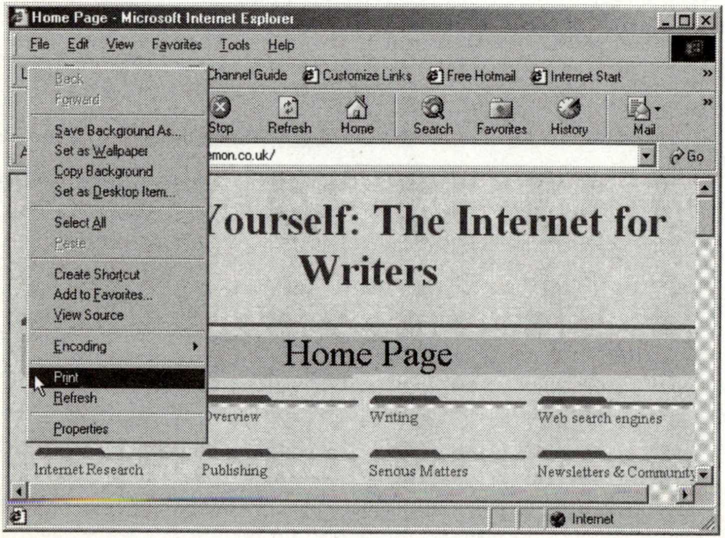

Print links from a Web page

Click .

Select **Print table of links** for a list of links on the Web page.

And/Or

Select **Print all linked documents** to print all the pages the Web page links to.

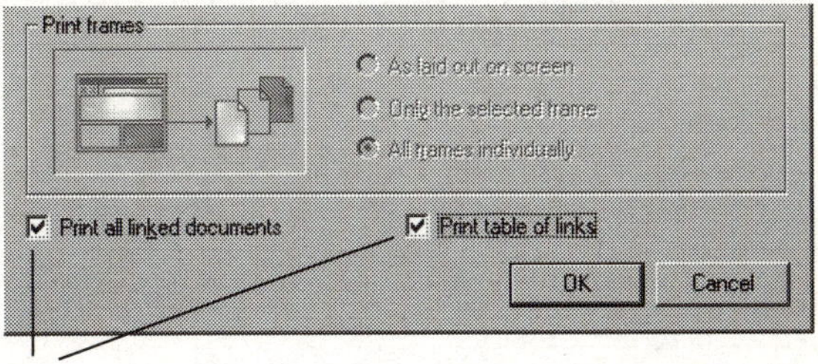

Chose as required

tip

Take care with the second option. If the Web page has many links you could be printing for a long time.

Preview a Web page before printing

1. In the **File** menu, click on **Print Preview**.

2. Choose commands from the toolbar to preview and print the Web page.

tip

You can add a Print Preview button  to your standard toolbar. See page 55.

Security

Use secure sites

'Secure' sites prevent unauthorized access to information that is sent to or from them by encoding it. Internet Explorer deals with this encoding for you.

A secure Web site automatically sends you a certificate guaranteeing its security and Internet Explorer then displays a lock icon on the status bar.

Internet Explorer can warn you if you are about to send information (such as your credit card number) to an unsecure or suspect site.

View security certificates

1. In the **Tools** menu click on **Internet Options…**

2. Click the **Content** tab.

3. Under **Certificates**, click **Certificates…** or **Publishers…** to view the list of current certificates that you trust.

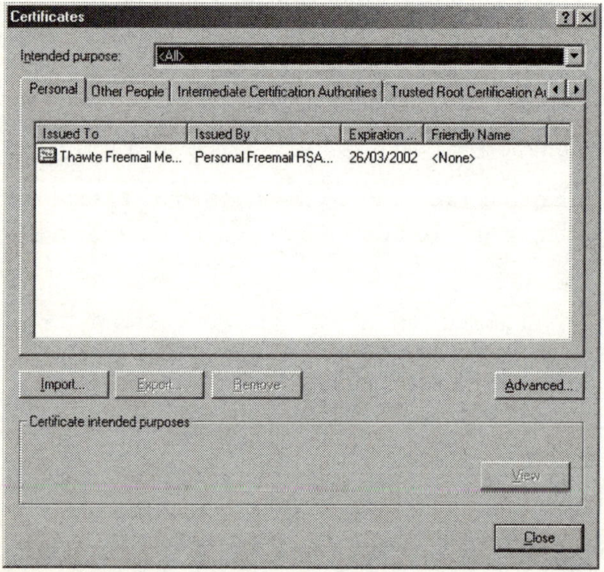

Obtain personal certificates

A 'personal certificate' to guarantee that you are who you say you are has a private key that only you know. You can use this to guarantee your identity when you send personal information to a Web site requiring this verification.

1. In the **Help** menu click on **Contents and Index**.

2. Under the **Search** tab type **Protection**.

3. Double-click on **Protecting your identity over the Internet**.

4. Click on the link obtain your personal security certificate.

Securely share personal information

Using Profile Assistant will save you entering the same information each time you visit a new Web site that requests it. This information is securely stored on your computer.

When a Web site requests information from Profile Assistant, the request will tell you:

- The Internet address of the site.
- What information is requested (you can exclude information if you require).
- How this information will be used.
- Whether you can verify the site's certificate over a secure connection.

Store personal information for Web sites

1. In the **Tools** menu click on **Internet Options…**

2. Click the **Content** tab.

3. Under **Personal information**, click **My Profile…** to view and edit information in **Profile Assistant**.

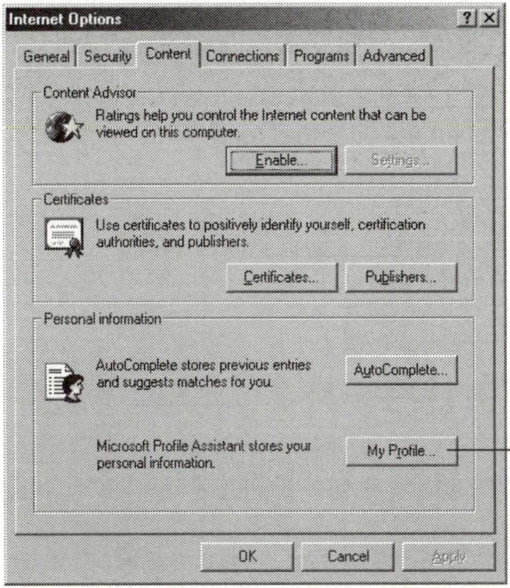

Click on My Profile…

Security zones

Internet Explorer can sort the Internet into differing security zones:

: Default zone. Default security level medium.

: Default security level medium. Sites addable.

: Default security level low. Sites addable.

: Default security level high. Sites addable.

tip

The right-hand side of the status bar shows icons for the zone you are viewing.

Set a security level for each zone

1. In the **Tools** menu click on **Internet Options…**

2. Under the **Security** tab click a zone icon.

3. Click **Default Level** to reset levels and enable the slider bar – up for increased security, down for decreased.

4. Click **Custom Level…** to alter levels in detail.

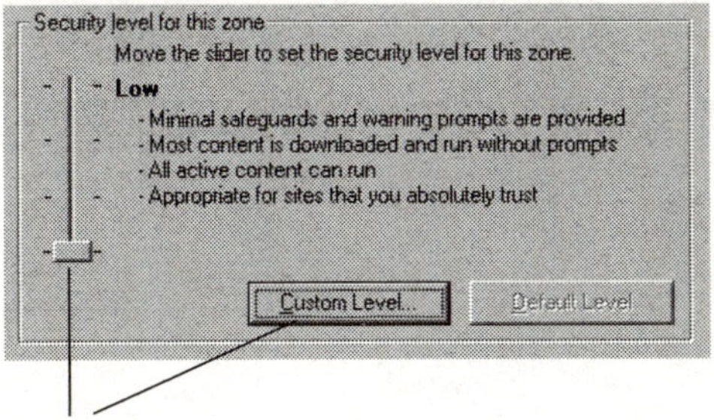

Alter as required

tip

Stick with the default level unless you are experienced.

Assign a Web site to a security zone

1. In the **Tools** menu click on **Internet Options…**

2. Under the **Security** tab click a zone icon.

3. Click **Sites…** then type the Internet address for the Web site to add to this zone.

4. If you clicked on the **Local Intranet** icon, click **Advanced** then type the Internet address for the site to add to this zone.

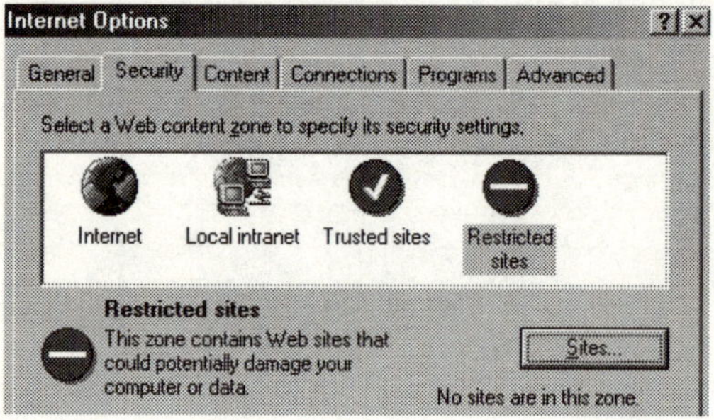

tip

Everything not assigned a zone or on your local computer is under the Internet zone. You cannot add Web sites to this zone.

Protect yourself from unsafe software

Downloaded malicious programs can damage your computer system.

The higher the security level the more warnings and prompts are displayed when software is downloaded before it can be saved or run. At the highest level very little can be downloaded and run.

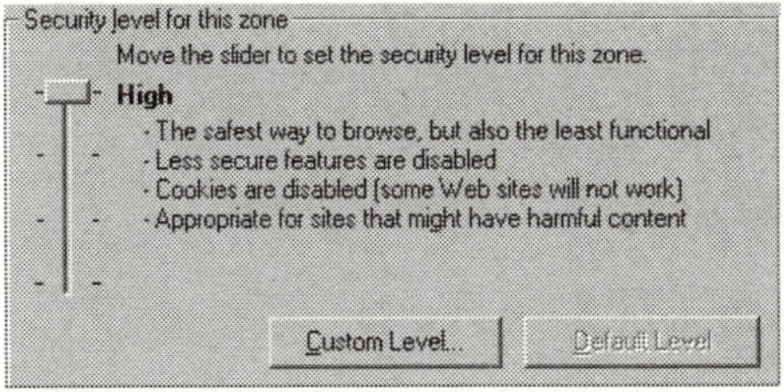

tip

Leaving settings at the default level should give you adequate protection.

Cookies

Some Web sites store a small text file on your hard disk called a 'cookie', containing information about you and how you view the site.

Cookies contain only information that you have made available by typing (your name, for instance) or by viewing (which pages you visited, for example).

A cookie file, viewed in Notepad

Customize handling of cookies

1. In the **Tools** menu click on **Internet options...**

2. Under the **Security** tab click a zone icon.

3. Click on **Custom Level...**

4. Scroll down to the **Cookies** icon in the **Security Settings** page and select your choice.

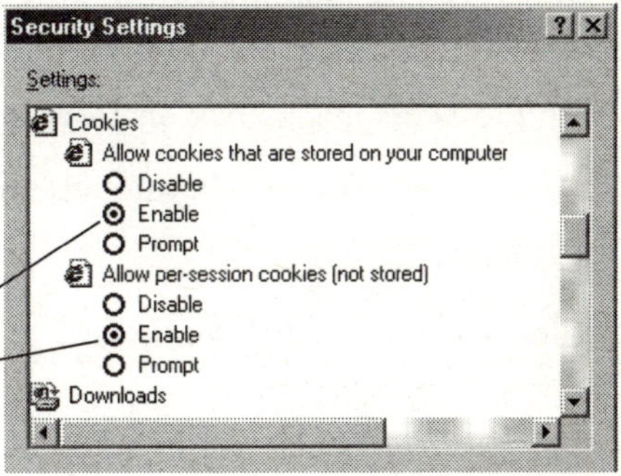

Set the cookie options

tip

If you click on **Start - Programs - Accessories - System Tools - Disk Cleanup** to tidy up your Temporary Internet Files folder, cookies will be left in the folder.

Safe viewing

Control access to Web sites

Content Advisor can control the type of site that may be accessed.

1. In the **Tools** menu click on **Internet Options…**

2. Under the **Content** tab, in **Content Advisor** select **Enable…**

Or

If already enabled, click **Settings…** and type your password.

3. Under the **Ratings** tab click the category to change and adjust the slider.

4. Click **OK** (you will be prompted for a password if one is not set).

Allow others to view restricted or unrated content

1. In the **Tools** menu click on **Inernet Options…**

2. Under the **Content** tab in **Content Advisor** select **Enable…**

Or

If already enabled, click **Settings…** and type your password.

3. To permit restricted content, click the **General** tab, and select the **Supervisor can type a password to allow users: to view restricted content** check box.

4. To permit unrated content, select the **Users can see sites that have no rating** check box.

5. Click **OK**.

Specify Web sites that others can always/never see

1. In the **Tools** menu click on **Internet Options…**

2. Under the **Content** tab in **Content Advisor** select **Enable…**

Or

If already enabled, click **Settings…** and type your password.

3. Under the **Approved Sites** tab, type the Internet address of the Web site, and choose **Always** or **Never** for access to this site.

4. Repeat for each site required.

5. Click **OK**.

Customizing

Change the home page displayed on start up

1. In the **Tools** menu click on **Internet Options...**
2. Under the **General** tab.
3. Choose your desired home page.

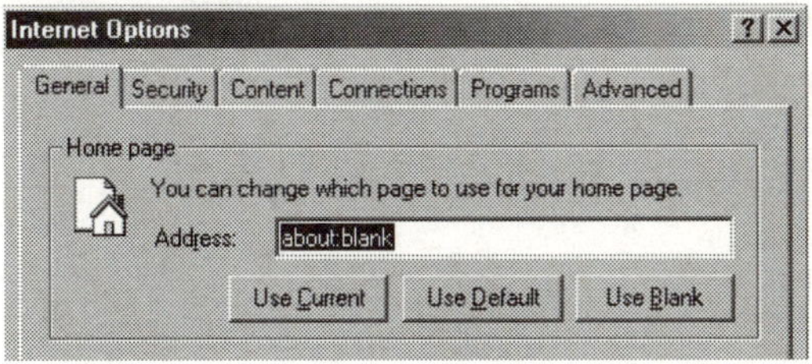

Choose which toolbars to display

1. Right-click on a toolbar.

2. Click on your choice from the list opposite.

A tick appears next to the toolbars displayed.

tip

Too many toolbars displayed at once reduces the area of the main window.

Customize toolbars

1. Right-click on a toolbar.
2. Click **Customize...**

   Toolbar buttons can be added and removed.

   The order of buttons may be altered.

   Different text and icon options are offered.

3. Click on **Close** when finished.

tip

If you click on the **Reset** button, it will put toolbars back to their default condition.

Reposition toolbars

The Address, Links and Radio bars can be moved by dragging to a different position.

1. Move the mouse cursor to just inside the vertical bar on the left of the toolbar.

2. The cursor will change to .

3. Left-click and hold – the toolbar can now be moved by dragging it.

Adjust toolbar width

When two toolbars are side by side:

1. Position the cursor over the vertical bar on the left of a toolbar.

2. The cursor will change to .

3. Click and hold – the cursor will change to .

4. Drag left and right to adjust width.

tip

Click » at the extreme right of a toolbar to see icons currently not visible.

Create a new toolbar

1. Right-click on the Windows taskbar, point to **Toolbars** and click **New Toolbar…**

2. Type the path to the folder or the Web site address you want as a toolbar, or select it from the list.

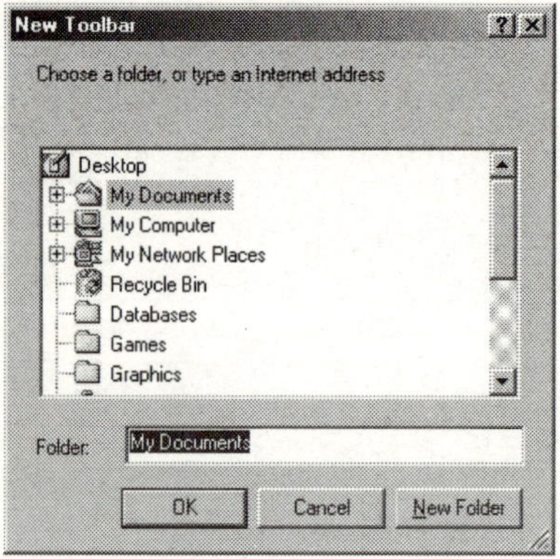

tip

You can make a folder containing Web links and program shortcuts, and turn the folder into a toolbar. It can be dragged to your desktop and resized.

Add links to the Links bar

1. If the Links bar is not in view right-click a toolbar and select **Links**.

2. Click on .

3. Drag a site from **Favorites** and drop it on the **Links** bar.

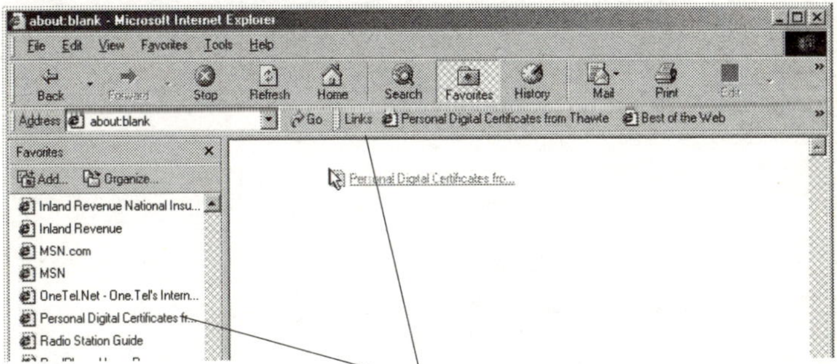

Drag from the Favorites to the Links bar

Change the order in the Links bar

1. Click and hold on the link you wish to move.

2. Drag it left or right on the Links bar.

3. Release when the vertical line is between the links where you wish to relocate it.

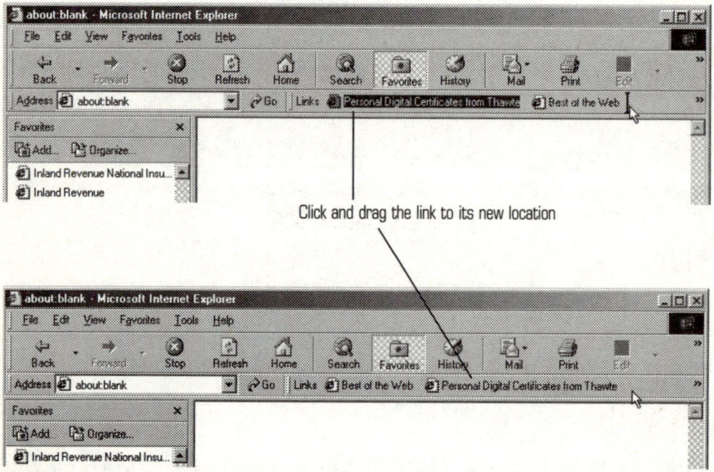

Remove a link from the Links bar

1. Right-click on the link.

2. Click **Delete**.

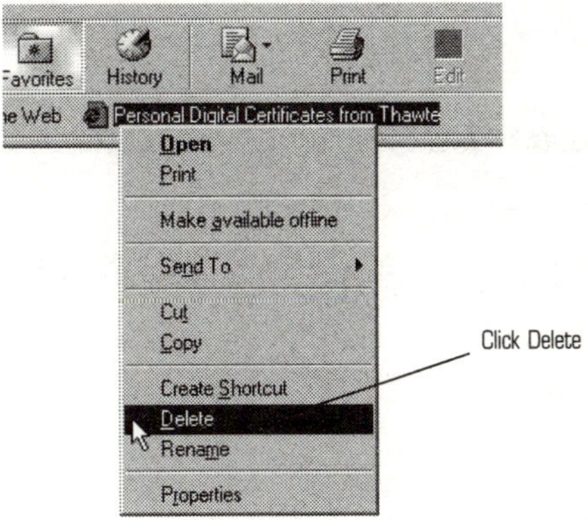

tip

The link is sent to the **Recycle Bin** and can be recovered if you make a mistake.

Change Internet Explorer display

You can change the way that Web sites are displayed on your screen.

Display Web page text in a different font

1. In the **Tools** menu click on **Internet Options…**

2. Under the **General** tab, click **Fonts**.

3. In the **Web page font:** and **Plain text font:** lists, click the required fonts.

tip

This will only alter default fonts. To change *all* fonts displayed see page 64.

Change Web page colours

1. In the **Tools** menu click on **Internet Options...**

2. Under the **General** tab, click **Colors...**

3. Change the settings as required.

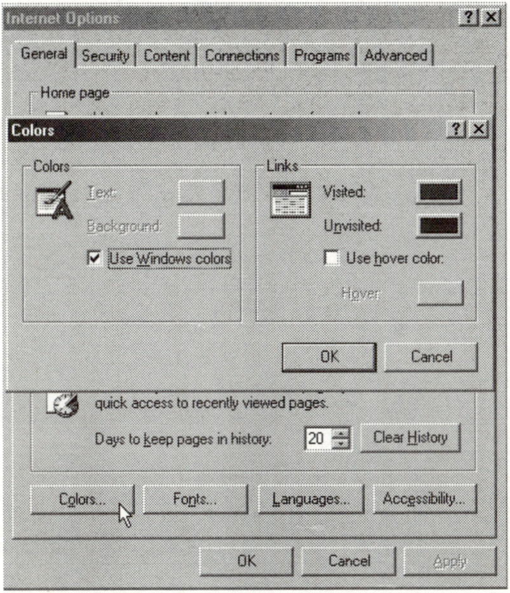

Specify fonts and colours to always use for Web pages

Having changed your font and colour settings as previously described you can force Internet Explorer to display them this way – regardless of what the designer of the site chose.

1. In the **Tools** menu click **Internet Options…**

2. Under the **General** tab click **Accessibility…**

3. Change the settings as needed.

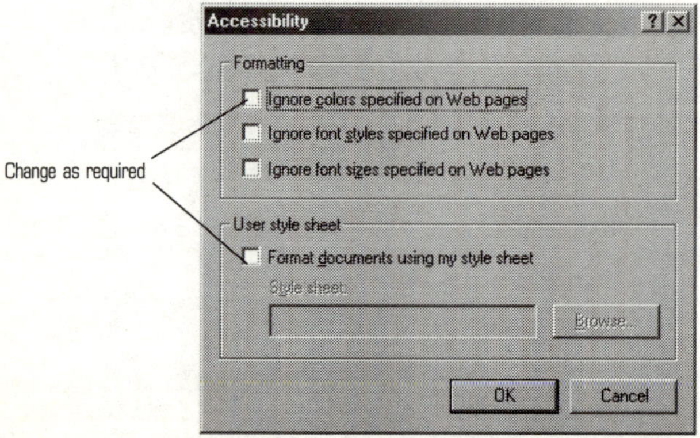

Display Web page text larger or smaller

1. In the **View** menu, point to **Text Size**.

2. Click the size you want from the menu.

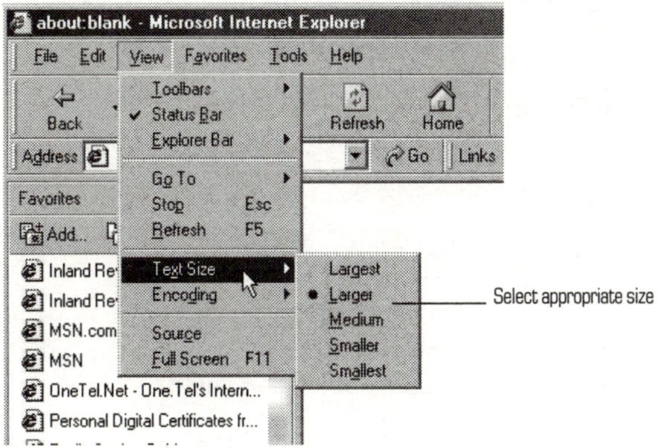

Display other language Web pages automatically

Most Web pages tell Internet Explorer what language is used. If this information is missing and you have Language Encoding Auto-Select enabled, your browser will automatically select the correct language.

1. In the **View** menu point to **Encoding**.

2. If **Auto-Select** has no check mark, click it.

tip

If you are missing some components that support the language you will be given the chance to download them.

Set the language for pages manually

If Auto-Select cannot determine the correct language and you know what it should be:

1. In the **View** menu, point to **Encoding**.

2. Point to **More** and then click the appropriate language.

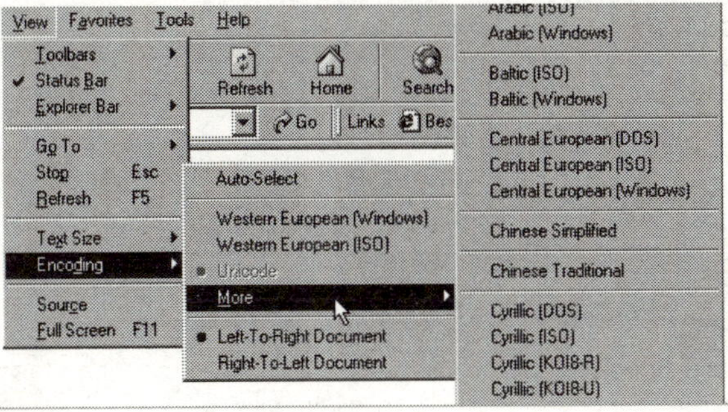

tip

In the **Tools** menu click on **Internet Options...** and under the **Advanced** tab in the **Browsing** section, select **Enable Install On Demand**. This will then prompt you when fonts need to be added to display a language.

Specify another language for Web page content

To view multi-language Web sites in your preferred language, you can add to your languages list.

1. In the **Tools** menu, click on **Internet Options…**

2. Under the **General** tab, click **Languages**.

3. Click on **Add…**

4. Select the language to add.

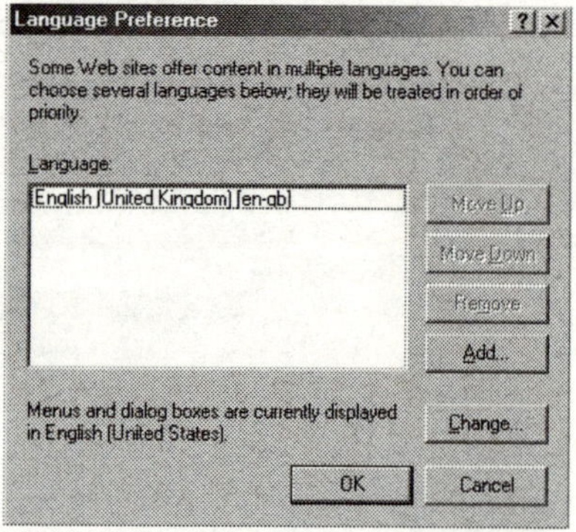

tip

You can specify the order of priority of languages. Multi-language Web sites will be displayed in the highest priority language.

Alter space used for Temporary Internet files

As you view Web pages, files are stored in the Temporary Internet Files folder to speed up the display.

1. In the **Tools** menu click on **Internet Options…**

2. Under the **General** tab click **Settings…**

3. Move the slider right/left to increase/decrease space used on your disk.

tip

You can change the way Web pages are updated in this dialog box.

Use keyboard shortcuts

1. In the **Help** menu click on **Contents and Index**.
2. In the **Index** keyword box type **shortcut keys**.
3. Double click **Internet Explorer** in the list.
4. Select your required topic for display.

tip

Learning keyboard shortcuts will save you mouse-clicks.

OUTLOOK EXPRESS 5

Introduction

Main Window

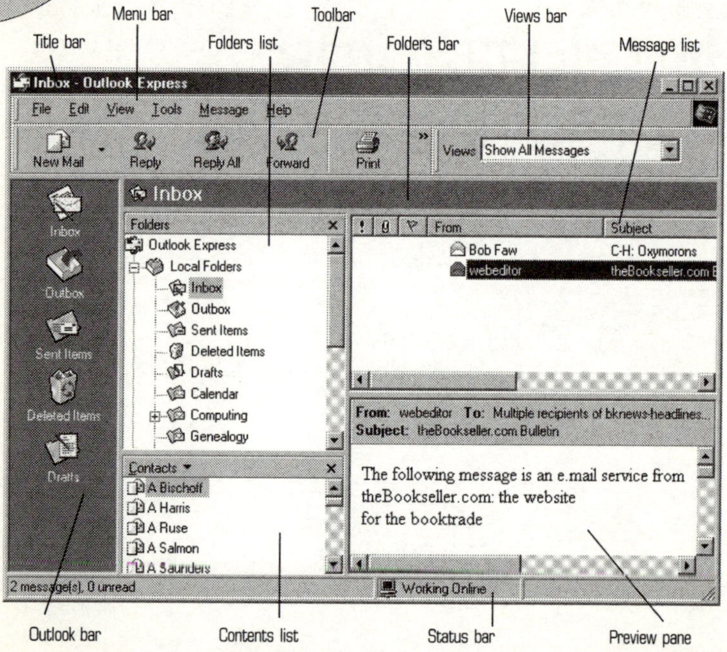

Setup

From your Internet service provider (ISP) or local area network (LAN) administrator get the following information:

Mail: mail server type (POP3, IMAP, or HTTP); your account name and password; incoming mail server name and (for POP3 and IMAP) outgoing mail server name.

News: news server name; your account name and password (if required).

tip

Write this information down somewhere safe in case you need it again.

Add a mail or news account

1. In the **Tools** menu click **Accounts.**

2. In the **Internet Accounts** dialog box click **Add…**

3. Select either **Mail…** or **News…** and follow the wizard's instructions.

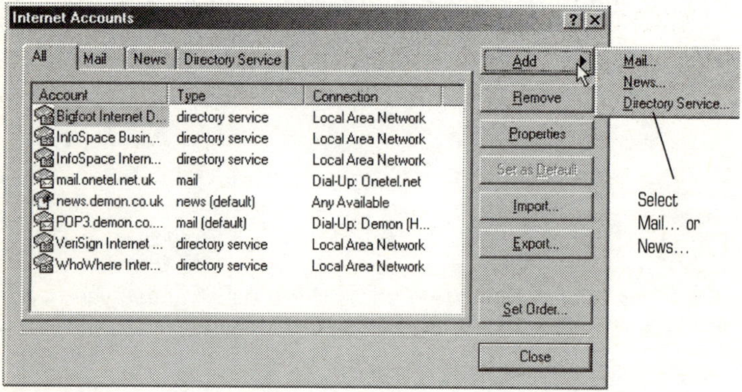

Change an existing server

1. In the **Tools** menu, click **Accounts...**

2. Under either the **Mail** or the **News** tab, click a server and then click **Properties**.

3. Change the information as required.

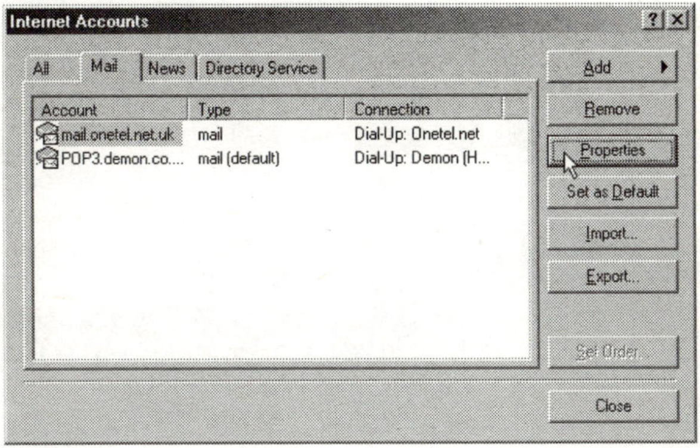

tip

If you have trouble connecting click the **Advanced** tab and increase the **Server Timeouts** setting.

Switch between mail and news reading

In the **Folders** list, click on Inbox or one of your own mail folders to go to your e-mail, or click a news server name or specific newsgroup to visit newsgroups.

Or

1. Click Outlook Express at the top of the **Folders** list.
2. Click the required link in the start-up pane.

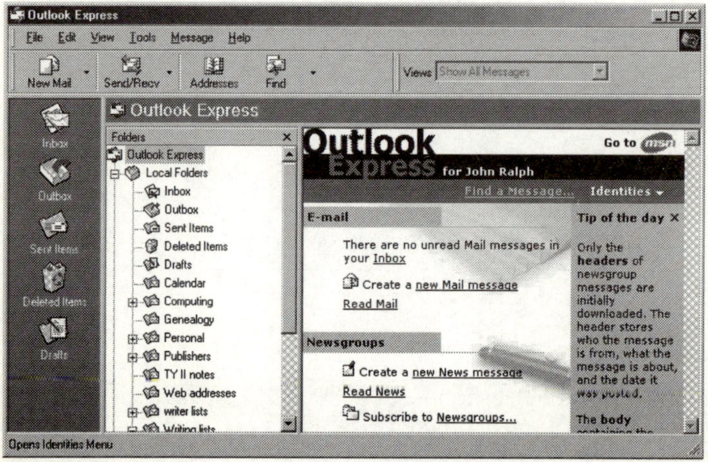

Open Internet Explorer from Outlook Express

1. In the **Help** menu, point to the **Microsoft on the Web** icon.

2. Click the Web option you want from the list below.

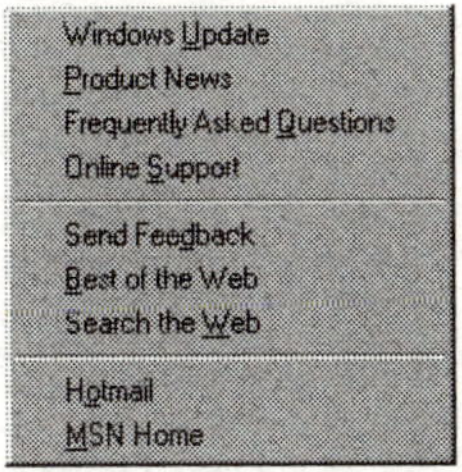

Use Outlook Express from your Web browser

Select Outlook Express as your default.

e-mail program and it will open whenever you click an e-mail link on a Web page or select the mail command in your browser or newsreader.

newsreader and it will open whenever you click a newsgroup link on a Web page or select the newsreader command in your browser.

1. In the **Tools** menu, click on **Options...**

2. Under the **General** tab, in the **Default Messaging Programs** area, click on **Make Default** for news and/or mail.

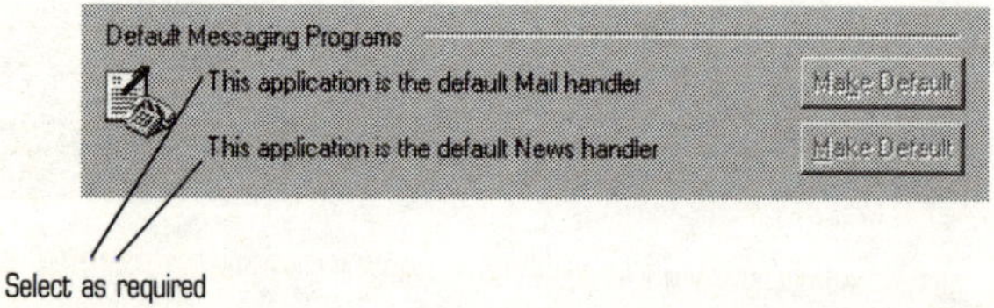

E-Mail

To begin a basic e-mail

Click  on the toolbar.

Or

Hold down **CTRL** and press **N**.

Or

In the **File** menu point to **New** and click on **Mail Message**.

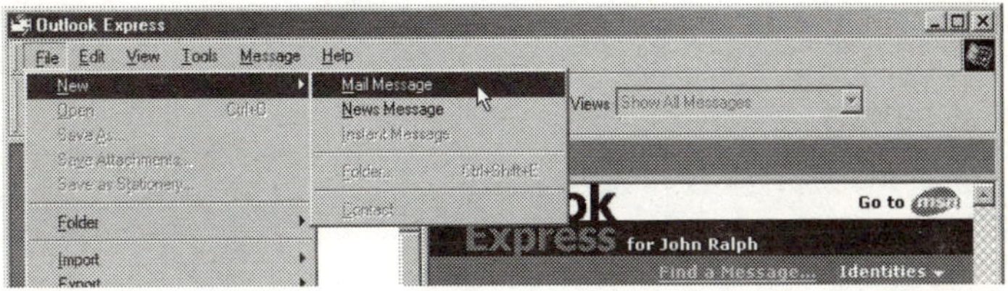

New Message window

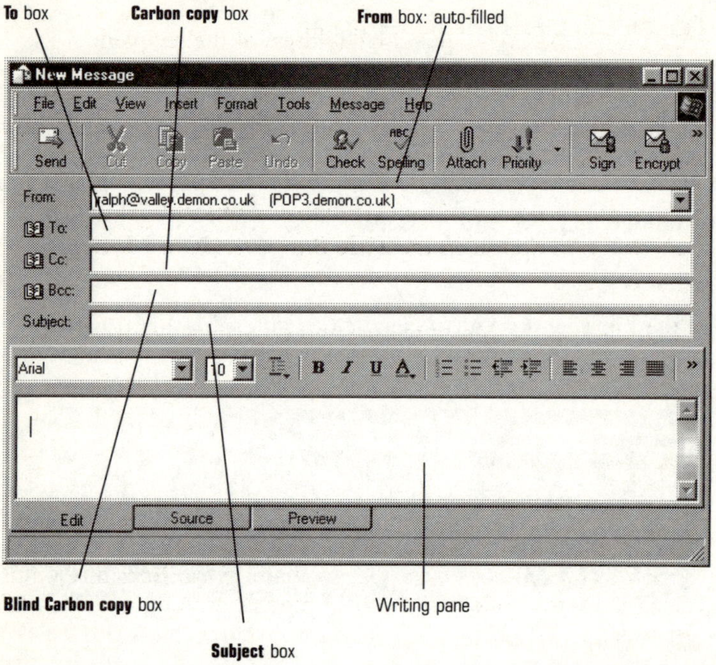

Address e-mail

1. The **From:** box is automatically filled with your address.

2. In the **To:** box type the e-mail address of the recipient.

3. To send copies to more than one recipient: in the **Cc:** and/or the **Bcc:** boxes type the addresses of each recipient separated by a comma or a semi-colon.

4. Type the name of your message in the **Subject** box. (This name will now appear in the **Title Bar** of the **New Message** window.)

5. Left-click in the **Message area** and type your message.

tip

With **Carbon copy (Cc:)** recipients see who else has received the message; with **Blind carbon copy (Bcc:)** the message appears to have been sent just to them. If the **Bcc:** box is not displayed, select **View** in the new message menu and click **All Headers**.

Send mail immediately

1. After composing your message click 

on the **New Message** toolbar.

2. If you are connected the mail will be sent immediately. If you are offline and close Outlook Express you will be asked if you wish to go online to send the mail.

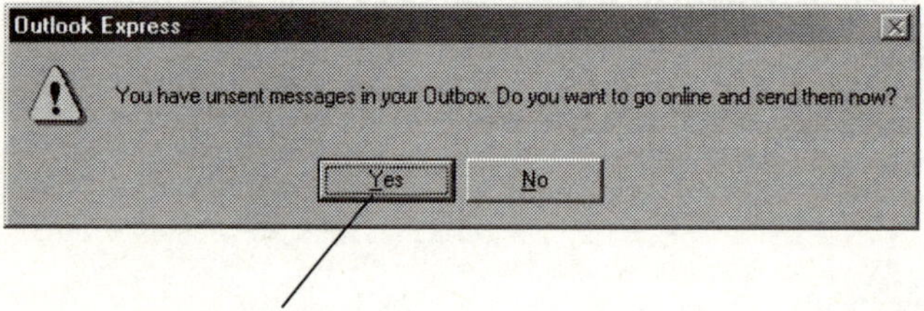

Click Yes to send your mail

Send mail later, if composing offline

1. In the **File** menu in the **New Message** window select **Send Later**.

2. Your mail will be saved in the Outbox.

3. If you then close Outlook Express you will be asked if you wish to go online to send the mail.

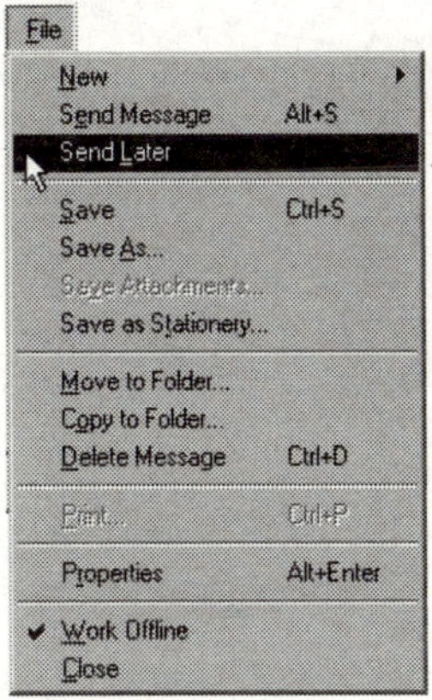

Click on Send Later

Save an e-mail to work on later

1. In the **File** menu in the **New Message** window select **Save.**

2. A message box will appear telling you that your message is now saved in the Drafts folder.

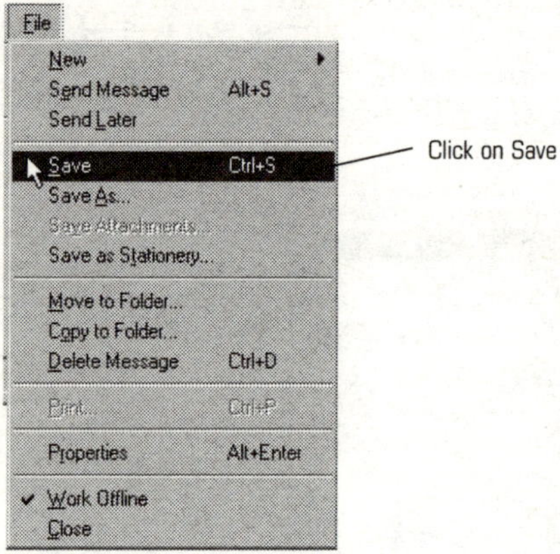

tip

If you leave the **Don't show me this again** checkbox unchecked, you will be reminded where your e-mail has been stored each time you save it.

Save e-mail to any folder on your disk

1. In the **File** menu in the **New Message** window select **Save As...**

2. The dialog box that appears offers a choice of formats, and a choice of disk and folder to save in.

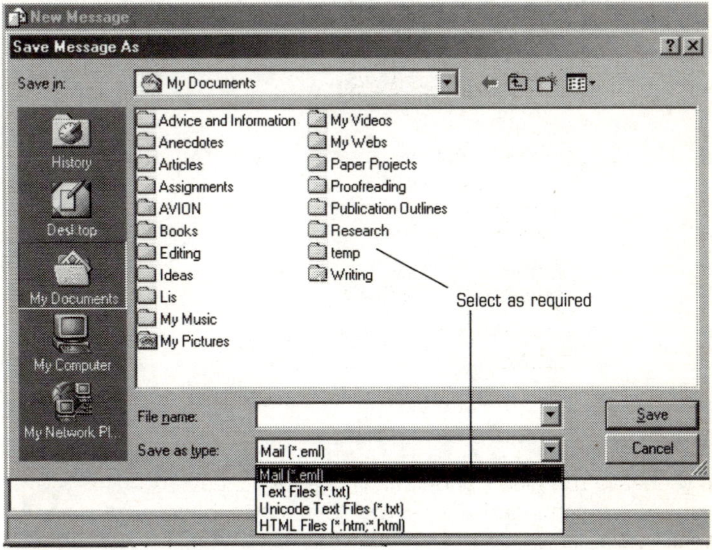

Receive e-mail

Outlook Express will automatically download your email on first connecting during a session. To download further e-mail at any time:

1. Click  on the toolbar.

Or

1. If you have more than one account, click the drop-down arrow beside  and select the account to use from the list.

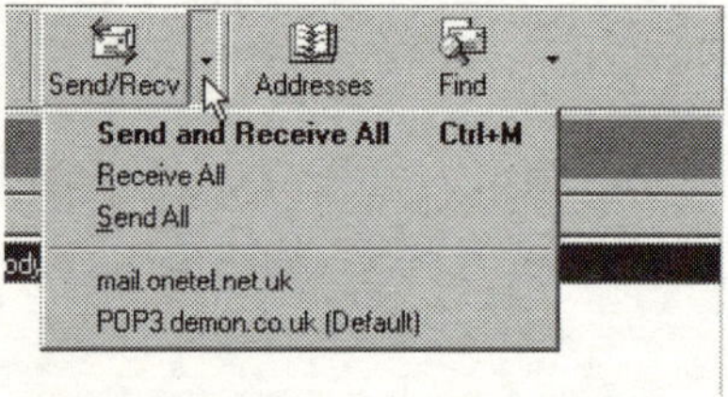

Read e-mail

1. Click the  icon in the **Outlook** bar or the  Inbox icon.

2. To view the message in the preview pane, click the message in the message list.

3. To view the message in a separate window, double-click the message in the message list.

tip

To see all message transmission details, in the **File** menu click **Properties**.

Save a message as a file

1. In the **File** menu, click **Save As...**

2. Select a format (mail, text or HTML) and a location to save the file in.

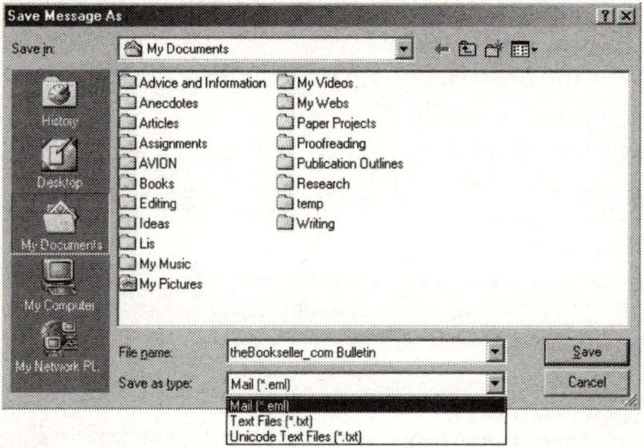

tip

If the message has been received in HTML format, saving it as text will lose any formatting such as background, colours and bullets.

View a file attachment

When a message has a file attached, a paper clip is displayed next to it in the message list.

1. In the preview pane, click the icon in the message header, and then click the file name.

Or

1. In the message window, double-click the icon beside the message header.

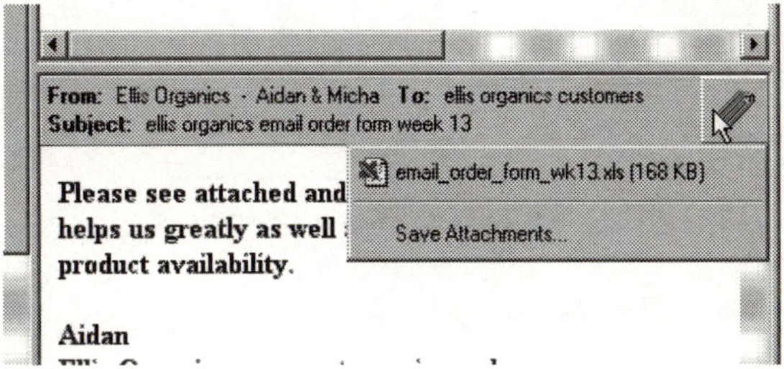

Save a file attachment

1. Click the message in the message window.
2. In the **File** menu, click **Save Attachments…**
3. Click the file name.

Or

1. Click the  icon in the preview pane.
2. Select **Save Attachments…** under the file name.

tip

If you save an attachment you can run a virus-checking program on it before opening it.

Read and send international messages

Outlook Express displays messages in the default language unless a message header specifies a particular language encoding. If information in the message header file is incorrect or missing this may not work.

To change the language encoding for a message you are reading:

1. Select a message.

2. In the **View** menu, click on **Encoding**.

3. Click the language required.

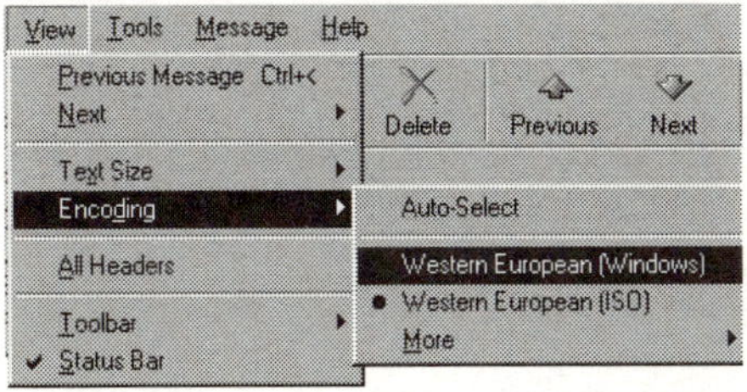

Set the default encoding for reading messages

1. In the **Tools** menu, click on **Options…**
2. Under the **Read** tab, click on **Fonts…**
3. Select a language and then click the **Set as Default** button.

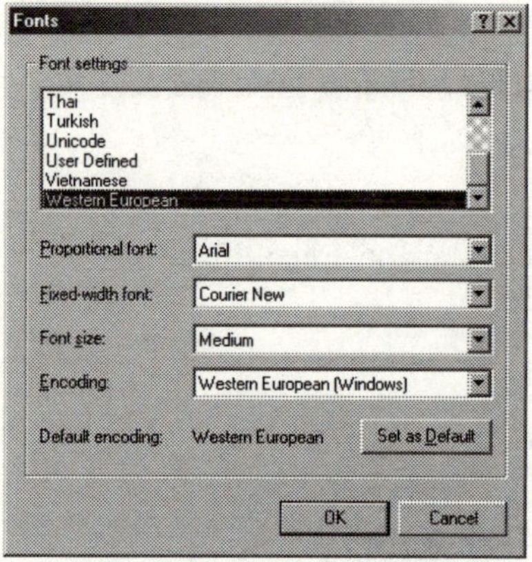

tip

Go to the 'International' area of the Internet Explorer Web site to get support for the language if you do not have it.

Group mail messages and their replies

1. Select a mail folder.

2. In the **View** menu, point to **Current View**.

3. Click **Group Messages By Conversation**.

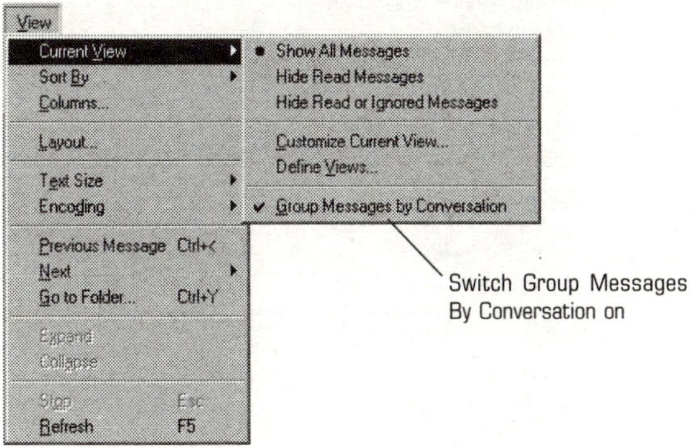

tip

Conversations are grouped according to the subject title of the original message. Replies are shown as 'RE: subject title'.

Expand grouped messages

1. In the **Tools** menu, click on **Options…**

2. Under the **Read** tab, click the **Automatically expand grouped messages** check box.

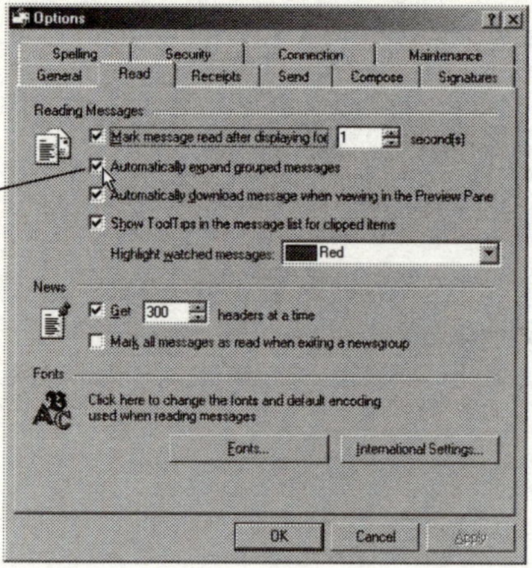

Click on Automatically expand grouped messages

tip

Clicking the + or the - sign to the left of the original message expands or collapses the group.

Forward a mail message

1. Select the message.

2. In the **Message** menu, click on **Forward**.

3. Type the e-mail name for each recipient, separating each name with a comma or a semicolon (;).

4. Type your message, and then click the **Send** button on the toolbar.

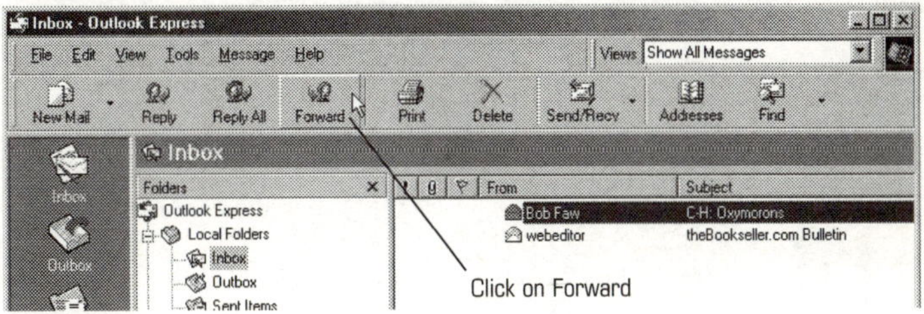

tip

If the **Forward** menu item or toolbar button is disabled, make sure you have downloaded the message body from the news or IMAP server.

Delete a mail message

1. In the message list, select the message.

2. In the toolbar, click the  button.

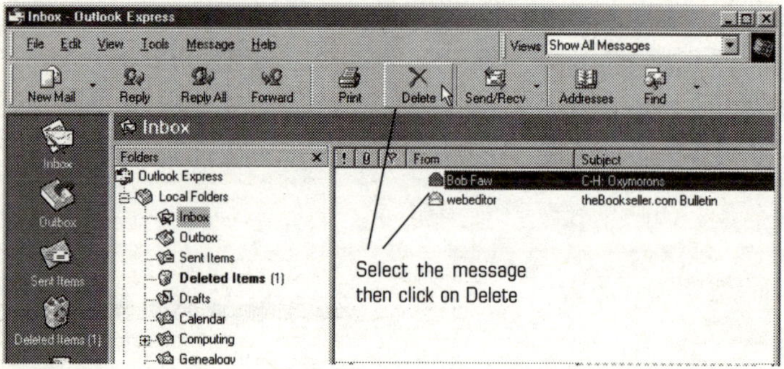

Restore a deleted mail message

1. Open the Deleted Items folder.

2. Drag the message to the required folder.

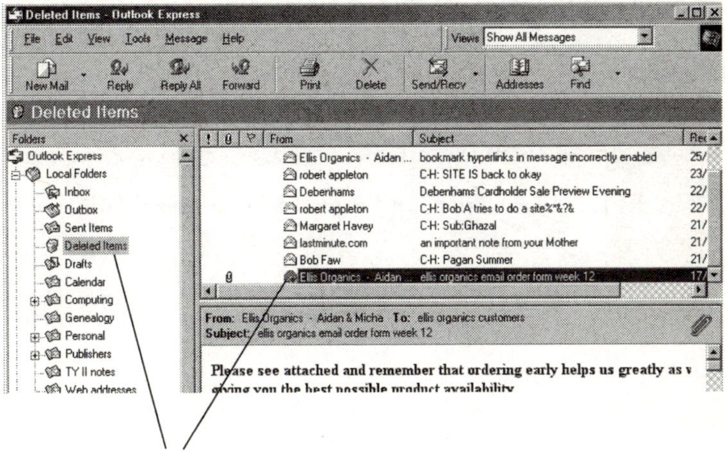

Open the Deleted Items folder then drag the message to the required folder

Clear the Deleted Items folder

Automatically

1. In the **Tools** menu, click on **Options...**

2. Under the **Maintenance** tab check the **Empty messages from the 'Deleted Items' folder on exit** check box.

Manually

1. Select the Deleted Items folder.

2. On the **Edit** menu, click on **Empty 'deleted items' Folder**.

Reduce online time

To keep line charges to a minimum when  is used:

1. In the **Tools** menu click on **Options...**

2. Under the **Connection** tab select **Hang up after sending and recieving**.

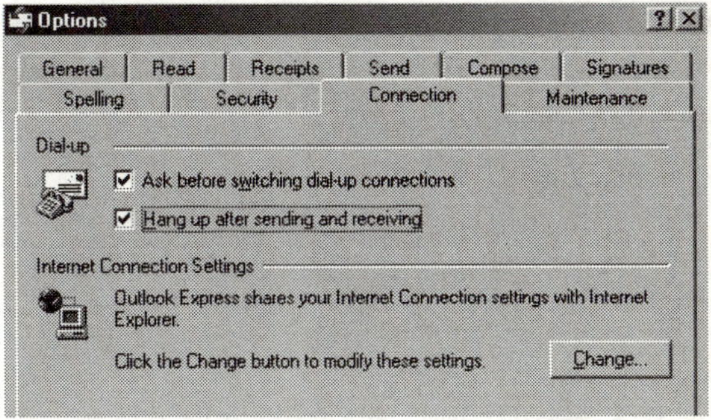

tip

If you have not checked **Work Offline** in the **File** menu and you select an IMAP folder while offline, Outlook Express will reconnect, and not automatically hang up.

Read messages while you are away from your Internet connection

1. In the **Tools** menu select **Options...**

2. Under the **General** tab, in the **If my computer is not connected at this time:** field, select **Connect only when not working offline**.

3. If using IMAP or HTTP server, click the server name in the folder list, ensure that the items to view offline are checked, and then click **Synchronize Account**.

4. On the **File** menu, click **Work Offline**.

tip

To find your account type, in the **Tools** menu click **Accounts...** Select your e-mail account and click **Properties**. The account type is listed under the **Advanced** tab.

Import e-mail

1. In the **File** menu, point to **Import**, and click **Messages...**

2. Select the e-mail program to import from, and click **Next**.

3. Locate your messages and click **Next**.

4. Choose **All folders** to import all the messages and click **Next**. (You can also choose **Selected folders:** to import messages from one or more folders.)

5. Click **Finish**.

tip

To find the name and version to import from, start the old e-mail program. On its **Help** menu, select **About**.

Request notification of receipt

In order to be sure that the recipient has seen your message you can request a receipt.

For an individual message:

1. In the **Tools** menu in the **New Message** window, click **Request Read Receipt**.

For all messages:

1. In the main window **Tools** menu, click on **Options...**
2. Under the **Receipts** tab select the **Request a read receipt for all sent messages** check box.

tip

If you do not want to send receipts, in the **Tools** menu click on **Options...** Under the **Receipts** tab, select the **Returning Read Receipts** option required.

Find mail messages in your message folders

1. In the **Edit** menu, point to **Find** and click on **Message...**

2. Enter your search criteria.

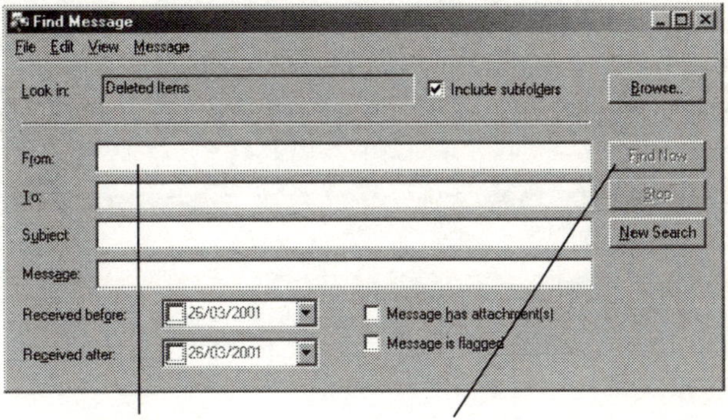

Enter your search criteria then click on Find Now

tip

Outlook Express searches only the current folder. To search in another folder, click on **Browse...** and select it.

Re-sort columns

You can find messages by re-sorting the columns in the message list.

Click the column heading to reorder the messages by that column. For example, clicking the **From** column will sort messages alphabetically by the sender's name.

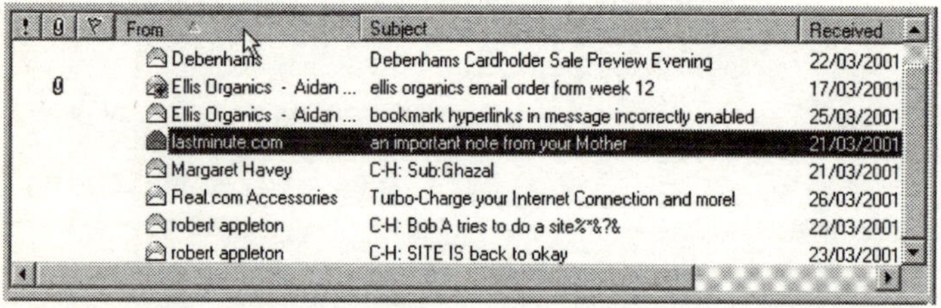

tip

Removing **Group Messages by Conversation** will fully sort the columns (see page 93).

Move or copy a message to another folder

1. In the message list, select the message.

2. In the **Edit** menu, click **Move to Folder…** or **Copy to Folder…**, and select the destination folder.

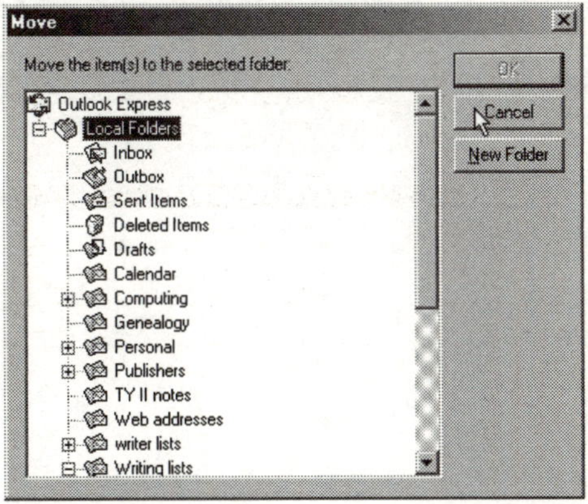

tip

You can also move a message by selecting it in the message list and dragging it to a folder in the folder list.

Add a folder

1. In the **File** menu, point to **Folder**, then click on **New**.

2. In the **Folder Name:** text box, type the name then select its new location.

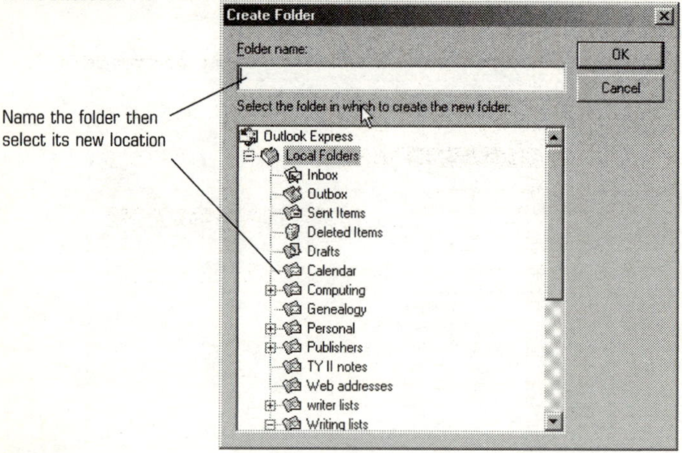

tip

You can add folders to the Inbox, Outbox, Sent Items, Deleted Items, and Drafts folders.

Delete a folder

1. Click the folder in the **Folders** list.

2. In the **File** menu, point to **Folder**, then click on **Delete**.

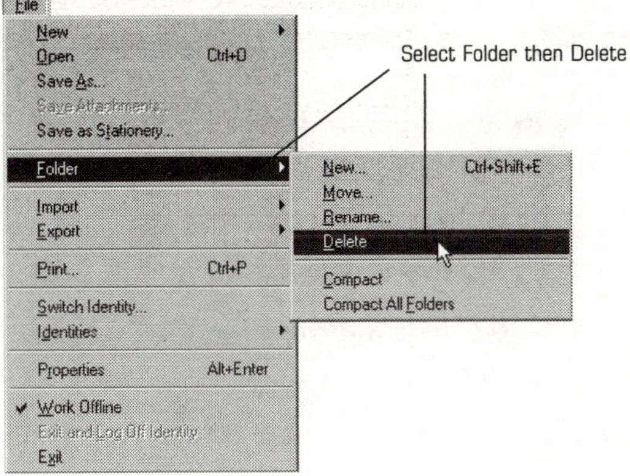

tip

You cannot delete or rename the Inbox, Outbox, Sent Items, Deleted Items, or Drafts folders.

Rules

If you have many incoming e-mails Outlook Express can help you sort them with rules. Message rules cannot be created for IMAP or HTTP mail accounts.

Create a rule for mail or newsgroup messages:

1. In the **Tools** menu, point to **Message Rules**, and click on **Mail...** or **News...**

2. Under the **Mail Rules** or **News rules** tab, click on **New** (go straight to step **3** if this is the first rule you are creating).

3. In the **1. Select the conditions for your rule:** section select at least one check box.

4. In the **2. Select the Actions for your rule:** section select at least one check box.

5. In the **3. Rule Description** section click the underlined hyperlinks to specify the conditions or actions for your rule.

6. If you enter multiple people or multiple words per condition, use the **Options...** button in the **Select People** or **Type Specific Words** dialog boxes for further customization.

7. In the **4. Name of the rule:** box, select the default name, type your new rule name, and click **OK**.

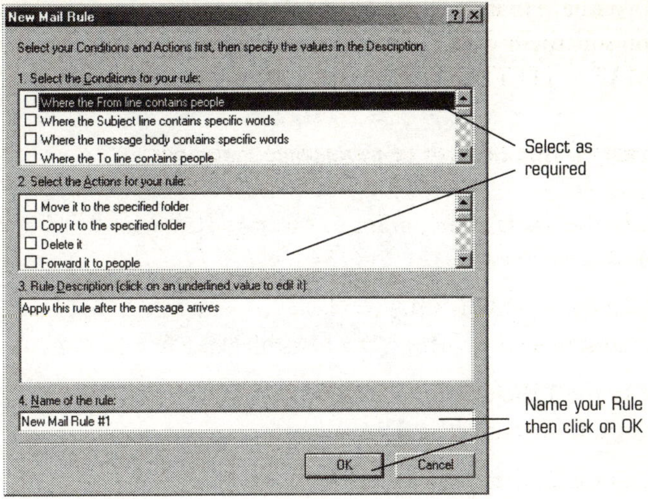

tip

You can create a new rule by selecting an existing one under the **Mail Rules** tab and clicking **Copy**. The copied rule can then be modified.

Create a rule from a message

1. Select a message in the main window.
2. In the **Message** menu click **Create Rule From Message...**

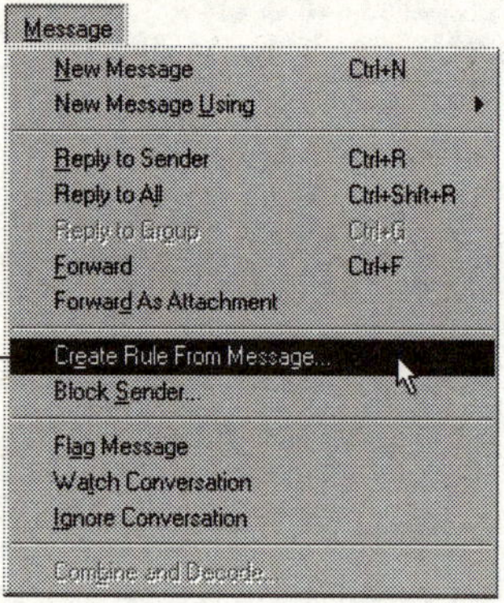

Click Create Rule From Message...

tip

Only the **Where the From line contains people** line is entered into the rule; all other conditions and any actions must be completed manually, as above.

Change a rule

1. In the **Tools** menu, point to **Message Rules**, then click on **Mail…** or **News…**

2. Select the rule and click **Modify**.

3. Make your changes in the **Edit Mail Rule** dialog box and click **OK**.

tip

You can rename a modified rule.

Apply a rule to downloaded messages

1. In the **Tools** menu, point to **Message Rules**, then click on **News…** or **Mail…**

2. In the **Message Rules** dialog box, click **Apply Now…**

3. Select the rules to apply, or click Select All to select all current rules.

4. Click **Browse…** to select the folders or newsgroups to which the selected rules are to be applied.

5. Click **Apply Now…**

tip

New rules are applied only to new, incoming messages.

Remove a rule

1. In the **Tools** menu, point to **Message Rules,** then click **Mail…** or **News…**

2. Select the rule.

3. Click **Remove.**

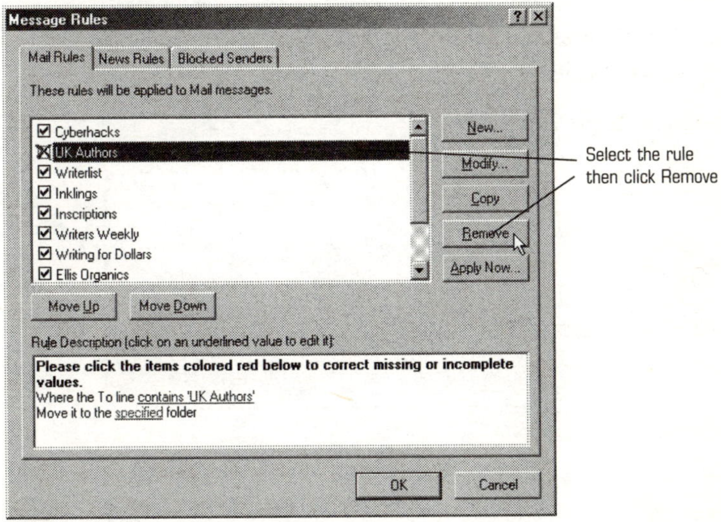

Change the font used to display messages

1. In the **Tools** menu, click on **Options...**

2. Under the **Read** tab click **Fonts...**, and make your selection.

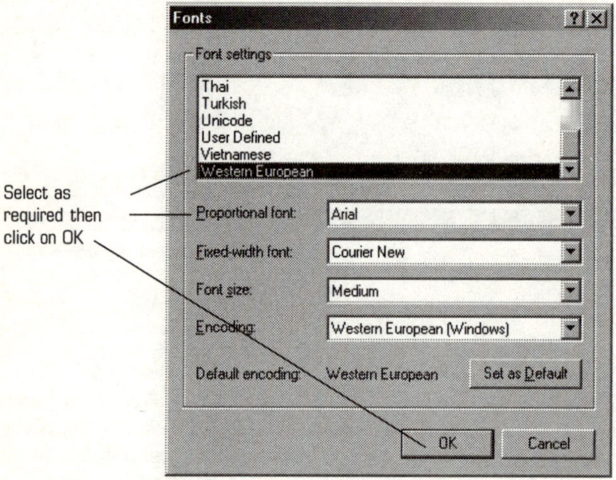

Format message text

Hypertext Markup Language (HTML) is the Web's standard for formatting text. Using it enables you to add bold and coloured text, bulleted lists, graphics, Web site links and more to your messages.

Only e-mail programs supporting Multipurpose Internet Mail Extensions (MIME) can read HTML messages directly. If your recipient's program does not read HTML, the message should appear to them as plain text with an HTML file attachment.

tip

To be certain that your replies can be read, in the **Tools** menu, click on **Options...** Under the **Send** tab, check the **Reply to messages using the format in which they were sent** check box.

Use HTML formatting generally

1. In the **Tools** menu, click on **Options...**

2. Under the **Send** tab, in the **Mail Sending Format** or **News Sending Format** sections, click on **HTML**.

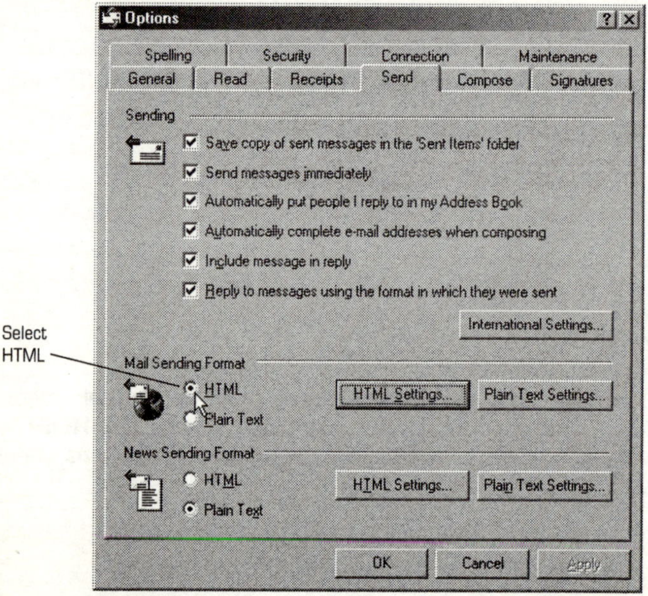

Use HTML formatting on an individual message

1. In a mail message window, click the **Format** menu.

2. Click alongside **Rich Text (HTML)** if a black dot appears by **Plain Text**.

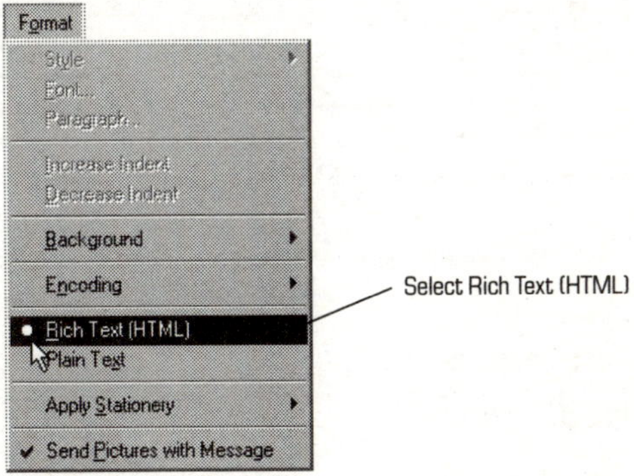

Edit an HTML message directly

1. In a new message window, click the **View** menu and ensure a check mark appears next to **Source Edit.**

2. Click the **Source** tab and edit the **HTML source code**.

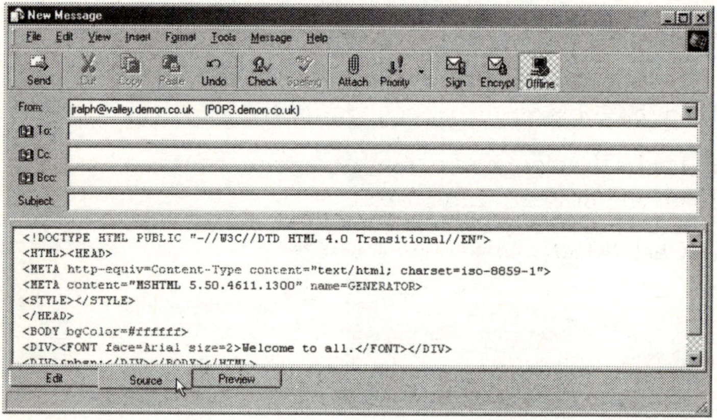

tip

HTML must be on for this facility. See above.

Use stationery with outgoing messages

When sending messages in HTML format, stationery (which can include a background picture, different text fonts and custom margins) can be used.

Apply stationery to all your outgoing messages

1. In the **Tools** menu, click on **Options...**

2. Under the **Compose** tab, in the **Stationery** area, select the **Mail:** and/or **News:** check boxes.

3. Click **Select...** and choose a design.

tip

Click **Create New...** to design your own stationery or **Download More...** to connect to Microsoft's Web page for extra stationery.

Apply stationery to an individual message

In the **Message** menu, point to **New Message Using**.

Or

1. Click the down arrow beside 
.

2. Select your stationery from the list.

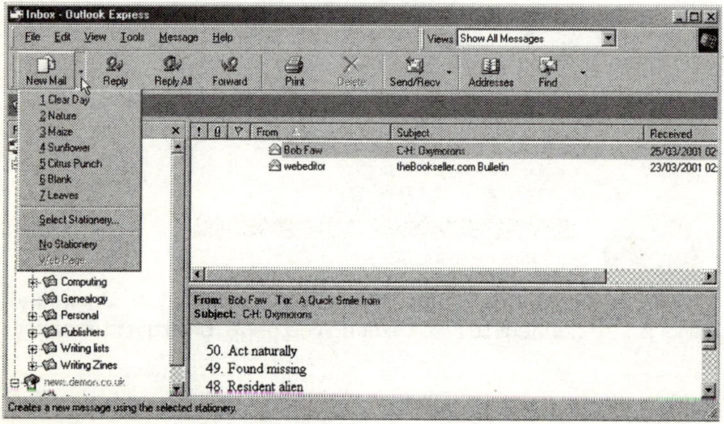

Apply or change stationery after starting a message

1. In the **New Message** window **Format** menu, point to **Apply Stationery**.

2. Select your stationery from the list.

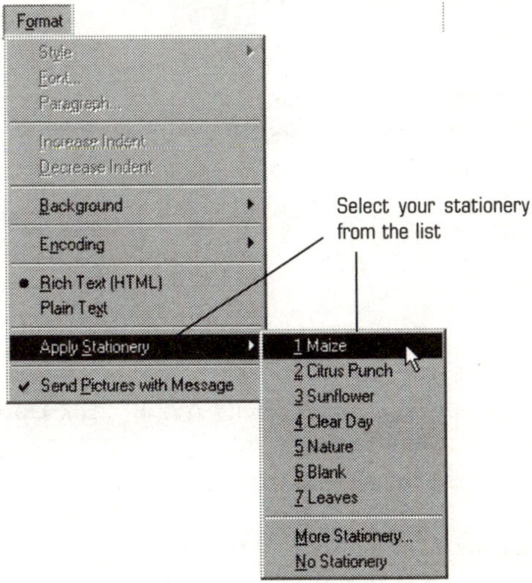

Check spelling

Outlook Express uses the spelling checker provided with Microsoft Word, Excel, and PowerPoint (Microsoft Office 95 and later). For those without Microsoft Office, spellcheckers are available at www.spellchecker.com.

In the new message window, click 

.

Or

In the **Tools** menu click on **Spelling…**

tip

To customize spelling, in the **Tools** menu, click **Options…**, and then select the **Spelling** tab.

Add a signature to all outgoing messages

A signature is a piece of text with which to end messages. It usually contains your name and any other information you care to include.

1. In the **Tools** menu click on **Options…**

2. Under the **Signatures** tab click the **New** button and then:

Enter text in the **Edit Signature** box to create a signature.

Or

Click **File**, and then find the text or HTML file to use.

3. Select the **Add signatures to all outgoing messsages** check box.

Use different signatures for different accounts

1. In the **Tools** menu click on **Options…**

2. Under the **Signatures** tab click the **Advanced…** button and then select the account to use the signature with.

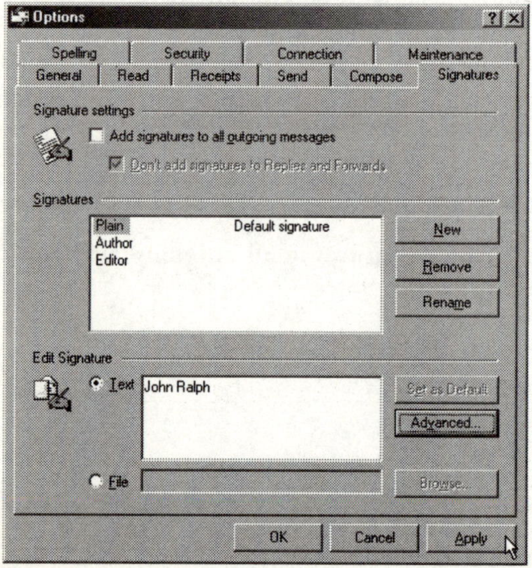

Use a signature only on individual messages

When you finish composing the message:

1. Ensure the **Add signatures to all outgoing messages** check box is clear (see page 123).

2. In the **Insert** menu, point to **Signature**.

3. Select a signature from the list if you have more than one.

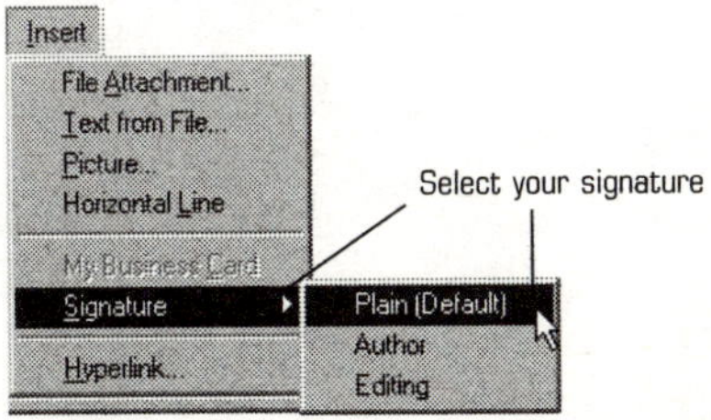

Insert a business card in all messages

A business card contains detailed information about you. It is like a long signature, invisible to you in your message, but available for the recipient.

1. In the **Tools** menu, click on **Options...**

2. Under the **Compose** tab, in the **Business Cards** section, select the **Mail:** or **News:** check box.

3. Select a business card from the drop-down list.

tip

To insert your business card, you must first create one. See page 242.

Add a business card to an individual message

1. In the **Insert** menu in a new message window.

2. Click **My Business Card**.

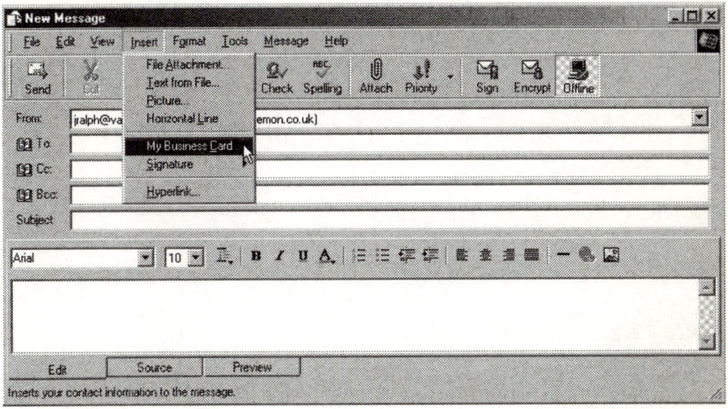

Change the priority of an outgoing mail message

To indicate the urgency of a message you can assign it a priority that the recipient can see.

Click the down arrow beside [Priority] in the new message window and select the priority required.

Or

1. In the **Message** menu in the **New Message** window, point to **Set Priority**.

2. Select the priority required.

tip

A high priority message has an exclamation point next to it ! ; a down arrow ↓ indicates low priority. Settings only apply to the current message.

Insert a file in a message

1. Click anywhere in the **New Message** window.
2. In the **Insert** menu, click on **File Attachment…**
3. Find and select the file to attach, then click **Attach**.

The file name will be shown in the **Attach:** box in the message header.

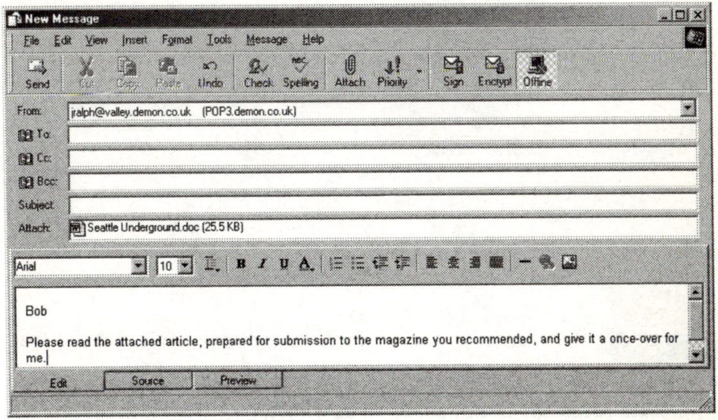

Insert a text file into a message

1. In the **Insert** menu click **Text from File...**

2. Find and select the text (.txt) file to add into the body of your mail message.

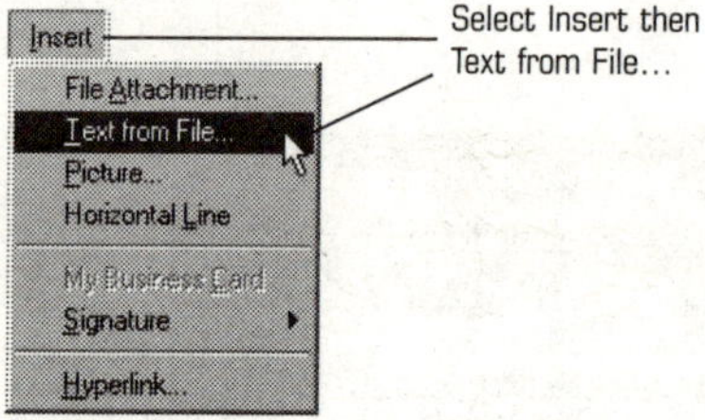

tip

Many people prefer to receive documents as text rather than as attachments, because of virus risks.

Include a sound in a message

1. Click anywhere in the message.

2. In the **Format** menu, point to **Background** and click **Sound…**

3. Enter the name of the file to include and the number of times to play the file.

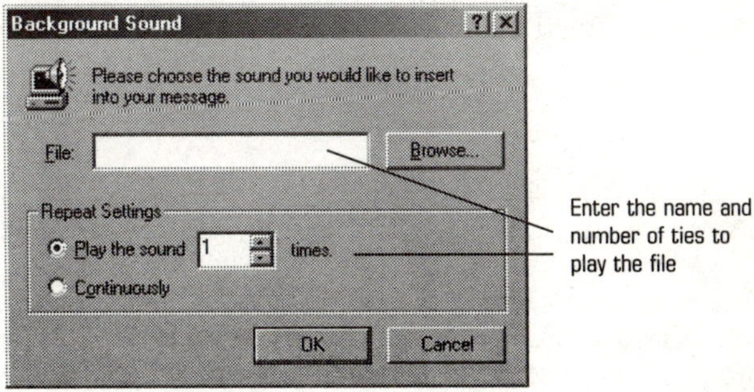

Insert a picture in a message

1. In the message, click where you want the image to appear.

2. In the **Insert** menu, click **Picture...** and then **Browse...** to find the image file.

3. Enter layout and spacing information for the image file as needed.

If you cannot select the **Picture...** command, make sure HTML formatting is turned on (see page 117).

tip

If recipients cannot see your inserted images, in the **Tools** menu, click on **Options...** Under the **Send** tab, click on **HTML Settings...** and make sure that **Send pictures with messages** is selected. Resend your message.

Insert a background picture in a message

1. In the **Format** menu in the new message window, point to **Background**.

2. Click **Picture…**

3. Click the **Browse…** button to search for the file to use.

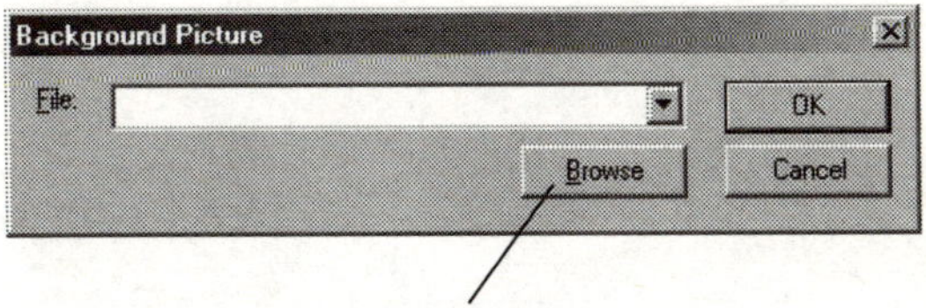

Click on Browse

Insert a hyperlink in a message

1. In the message, click where you want to add the hyperlink. (To create a hyperlink from text in the message, select the text before creating the hyperlink.)

2. In the **Insert** menu, click **Hyperlink...**

3. Select the file type, and then type the location or address of the link.

Select the file type and its location

tip

If you cannot select the **Hyperlink...** menu command, make sure HTML formatting is turned on (see page 117).

Insert an HTML page in a message

1. In the **New Message** window, click where you want to add the Web page.

2. In the **Insert** menu, click **Text from File…**

3. Change the **Files of type:** box to **HTML Files (*.htm,*.html)** and then find the file to add.

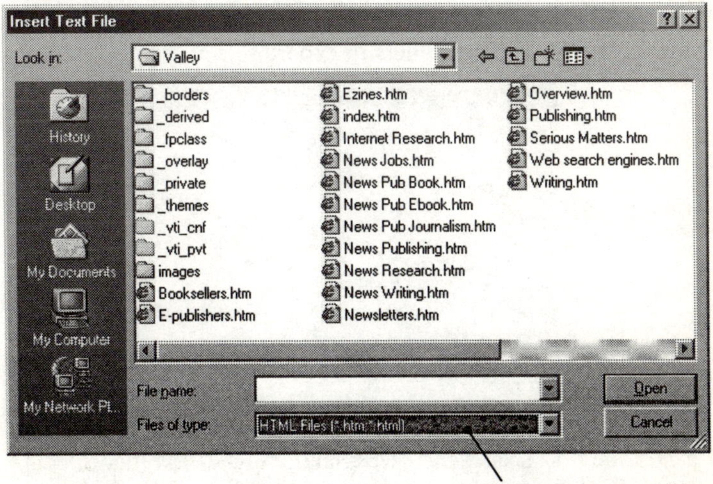

Change to HTML Files (*.htm, *html)

Export messages to Microsoft Outlook or Microsoft Exchange

1. In the **File** menu, point to **Export**, and then click **Messages…**

2. In the **Choose Profile** dialog box, choose the name of the program to export to.

3. To export all the messages, click on **All folders:**.

4. To export messages in one or more folders, click on **Selected folders:**, then select the folders to export.

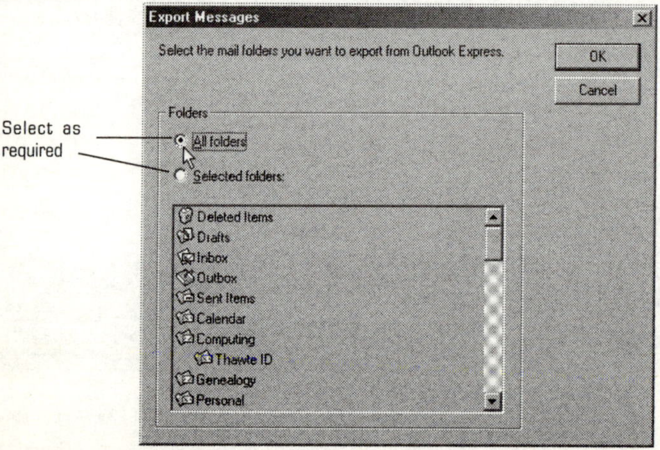

News reading

Subscribe to a newsgroup

When you add a news server (see page 174) you are prompted to subscribe to newsgroups on that server.

1. Click a news server name in the **Folders** list.

2. Click **Newsgroups…**

3. Select the newsgroup to subscribe to, then click **Subscribe**.

tip

You can double-click a name in the **Newsgroup** list for automatic subscription.

View a subscribed newsgroup

Click the name of the newsgroup in the **Folders** list

The newsgroup is displayed in the message and preview panes.

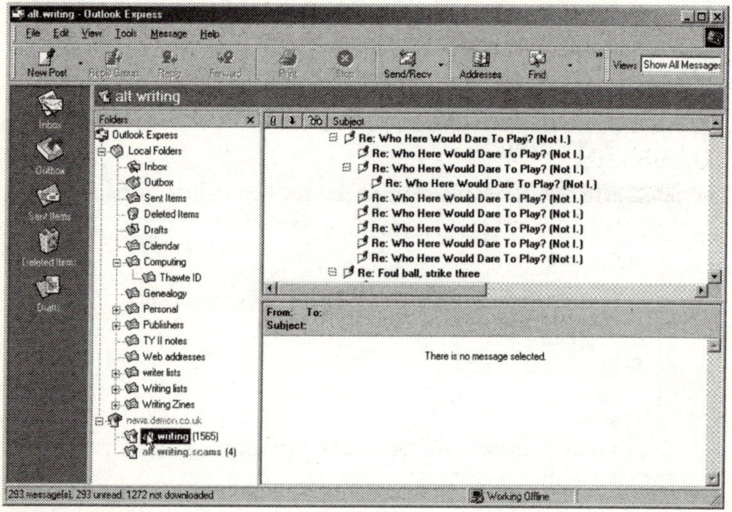

Cancel a newsgroup subscription

1. Click the news server name in the **Folders** list.

2. Click **Newsgroups...**

3. Under the **Subscribed** tab, select the group, and click **Unsubscribe**.

Or

1. Right-click the newsgroup in your **Folders** list and click **Unsubscribe**.

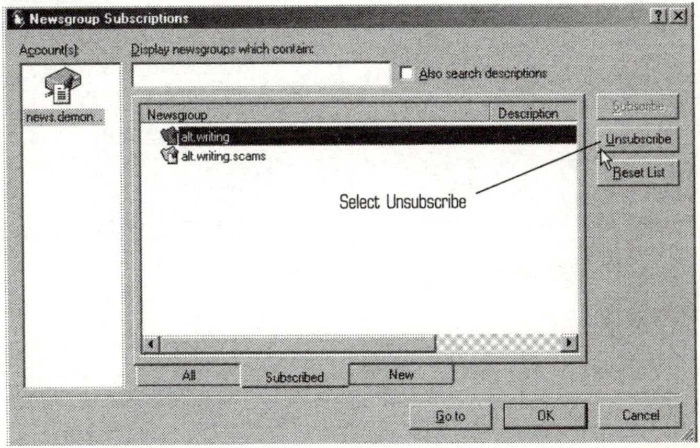

View a newsgroup without subscribing

1. In the **Tools** menu, click **Newsgroups...**

2. In the **Newsgroup Subscriptions** dialog box select the news server in the **Account(s):** list.

3. On the **All** tab select the newsgroup and click **Go to.**

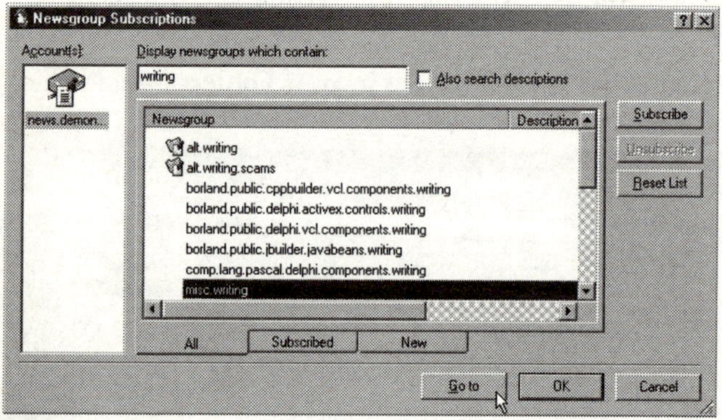

tip

Newsgroups you have chosen to view will appear in the **Folders** list. To subscribe after viewing, right-click the name and click **Subscribe**.

Find newsgroups of interest

You can search for keywords in newsgroup names that may indicate subjects of interest to you.

1. In the **Folders** list, click a server name, and then click the **Newsgroups...** button.

2. In the **Display newsgroups which contain:** box, type the words to search for.

tip

Not all news servers carry all newsgroups. If you are unsuccessful in your search you might try another server.

Read newsgroup messages

Outlook Express downloads only the headers of newsgroup messages by default.

1. Click a newsgroup in the **Folder** list.

2. Scroll through the message list for a message to read.

3. Click the message once to view in the **Preview Pane**.

Or

Double-click the message to view in a separate window.

tip

To display or change the preview pane, in the **View** menu, click **Layout...** and, in the **Preview Pane** section, select your option(s).

Reading individual newsgroup messages offline

1. While offline, select any headers of messages you wish to read.

2. In the Tools menu, point to **Mark For Offline**, and click **Download Message Later**. Repeat for each newsgroup with messages you want to read later.

3. When you go online, in the **Tools** menu, click **Synchronize All**. You may go offline after the messages are downloaded.

tip

To display just the messages selected for reading offline, in the **View** menu point to **Current View** and click **Show Downloaded Messages**.

Set up newsgroups for offline newsreading

1. From the **Folders** list, select a news server.

2. In the main window, select the subscribed newsgroup(s) to read offline (keep the **CTRL** key down while you click each newsgroup to select more than one).

3. Click **Settings...**, and then click:

All Messages

Or

New Messages Only (new since you last synchronized)

Or

Headers Only (subject, author, date and size of message).

4. Ensure newsgroups not to be downloaded are not checked.

5. Click on **Synchronize Account** to download.

Find messages in a newsgroup

1. While in a newsgroup, in the **Edit** menu, point to **Find** and select **Message in this Folder...**

2. In the **Look for:** text box, type the word(s) you want to search for, and click **Find Next**.

3. If your search returns too many results or fails, click the **Advanced find...** button and refine your search.

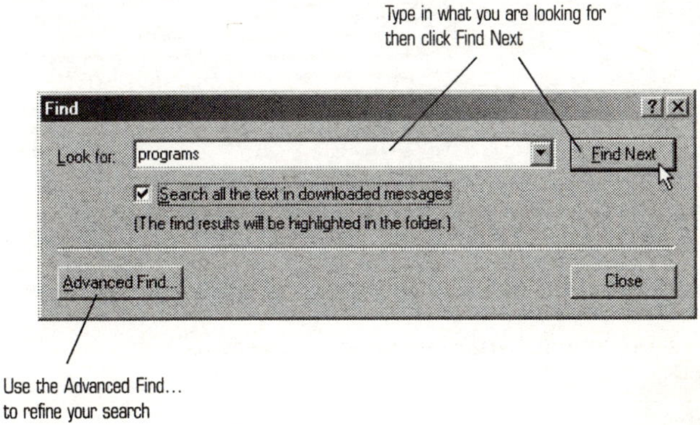

Re-sort columns

You can find messages by re-sorting the columns in the message list.

Click the column heading to reorder the messages by that column. (For example, clicking the **From** column sorts messages alphabetically by the sender's name.)

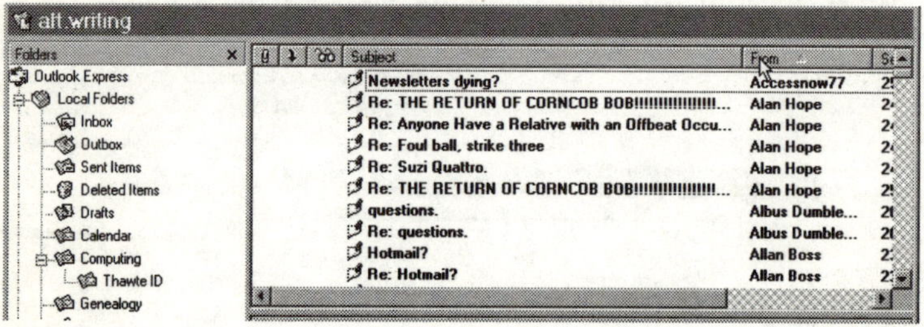

tip

Removing **Group Messages by Conversation** will fully sort the columns.

Post a newsgroup message

1. With a newsgroup selected in the folder list click **New Post.**
2. Compose your message.
3. Click on **Send**.

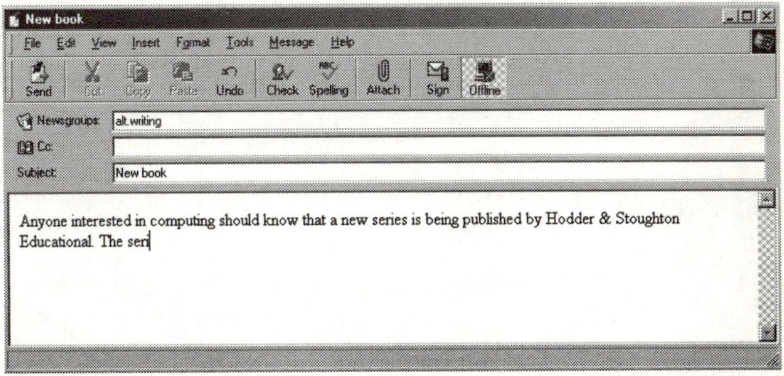

tip

If you forget to include a subject header you will be reminded.

Reply to a newsgroup message

1. In the message list, click the message you want to reply to.
2. To reply to the author by e-mail, click **Reply**.
3. To reply to the whole newsgroup, click **Reply Group**.
4. Type your message, and then click on **Send**.

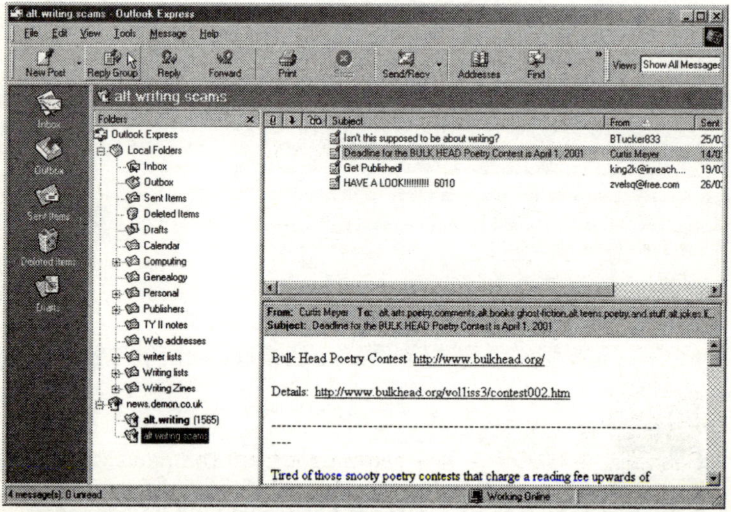

Cancel a message after it has been sent

1. Select the message.

2. In the **Message** menu, select **Cancel Message**.

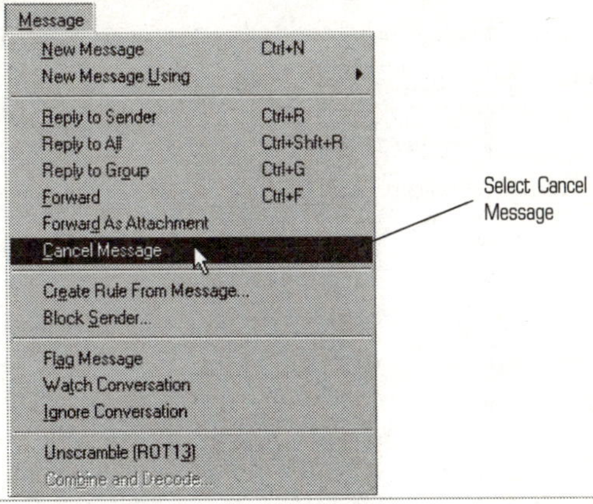

tip

Cancelling a message only removes it from the news server. If someone has already downloaded it before cancellation they will still have that message on their computer.

View newsgroup message information

1. Select the message.

2. In the **File** menu, click **Properties**.

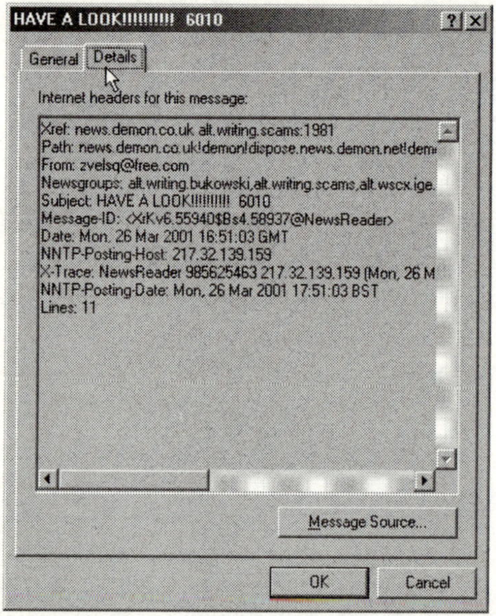

Send large messages

Some servers have restrictions on message size. Outlook Express can break one large message into several smaller ones to overcome this. It will recombine split messages when receiving them.

1. In the **Tools** menu, click **Accounts…**

2. Under the **Mail** or **News** tab, click on **Properties**.

3. Under the **Advanced** tab, select this check box:

and enter the maximum file size allowed by the server.

Set the line length in outgoing newsgroup messages

Some news servers do not display more than 80 characters per line. Outlook Express has a plain text default of 76 characters per line.

1. In the **Tools** menu, click on **Options…**

2. Under the **Send** tab, in the **News Sending Format** section, select **Plain Text**.

3. Click **Plain Text Settings…**

4. In the text box in:

type the number of characters per line to display.

> **tip**
>
> Replies usually add a highlighting character to each quoted line. Setting wrap length to 70 characters will avoid any reply quoting your text overlapping.

View only unread newsgroup messages

1. In the **View** menu, point to **Current View**.
2. Select **Hide Read or Ignored Messages**.

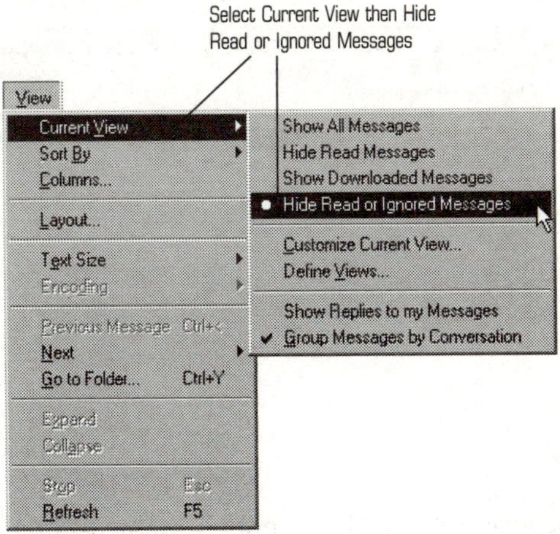

Watch a conversation

A message with its replies is called a conversation.

1. In your mail or newsgroup message list, select the conversation to watch.

2. In the **Message** menu, click **Watch Conversation**.

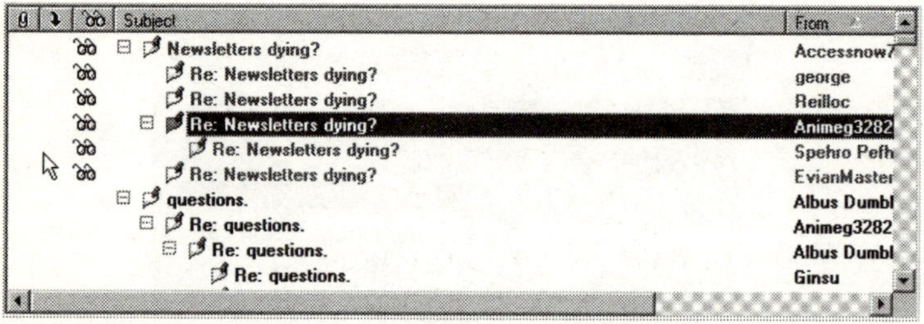

tip

If the **Watch/Ignore** column is turned on in your message list, the watch icon will appear next to all messages in a watched conversation.

Highlight watched messages

1. In the **Tools** menu, click on **Options...**

2. Under the **Read** tab, at the end of the **Highlight watched messages:** line, select a colour.

3. Click **OK**.

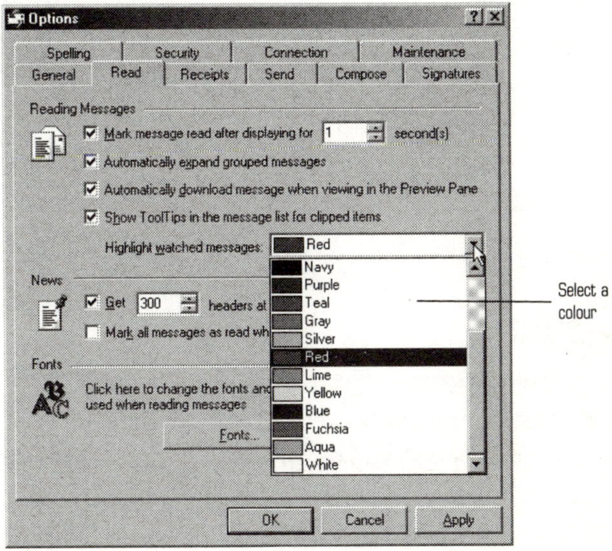

Ignore a conversation

1. In your mail or newsgroup message list, select the conversation to ignore.

2. In the **Message** menu, click **Ignore Conversation**.

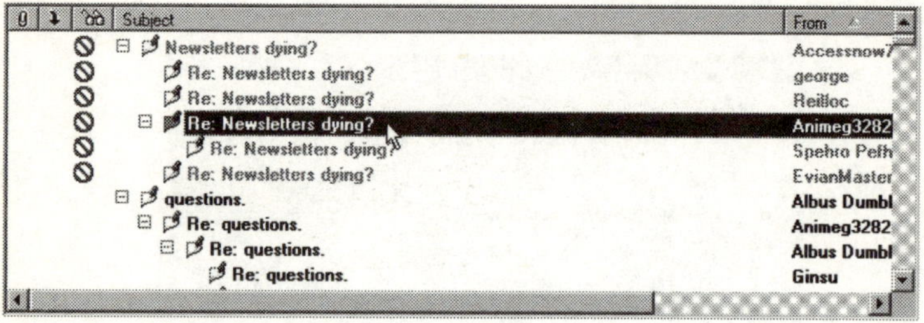

tip

If the **Watch/Ignore** column is turned on in your message list, the ignore icon will appear next to all messages in an ignored conversation.

Hide ignored messages

1. In the **View** menu, point to **Current View**.

2. Select **Hide Read or Ignored Messages**.

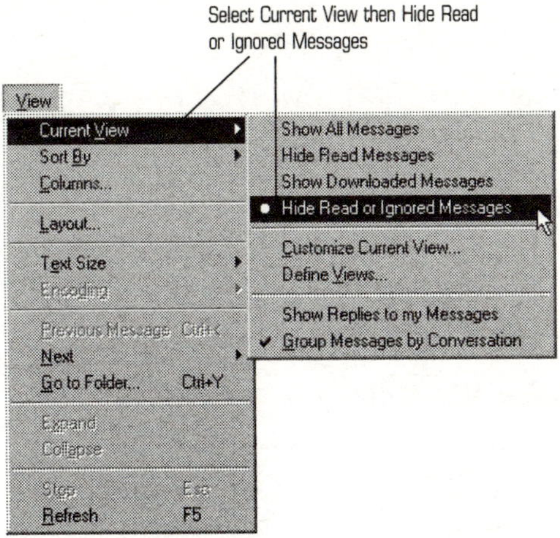

Hide ignored messages, but not read messages

1. In the **View** menu, point to **Current View**, and select **Hide Read** or **Ignored Messages**.

2. In the **View** menu, point to **Current View**, and select **Define Views...**

3. In the **Define Views** dialog box, click the **New** button.

4. In box 1 of the **View Editor**, ensure the **Where the message has been read** checkbox is cleared.

5. In box 2, click **Show/Hide** and select **Show messages**.

6. In box 3, give this view a name, and click **OK**.

7. In the **Define Views** dialog box, click **OK**.

View the replies to a message in a newsgroup

Click the plus sign (+) next to the message.

The replies to that message appear below it.

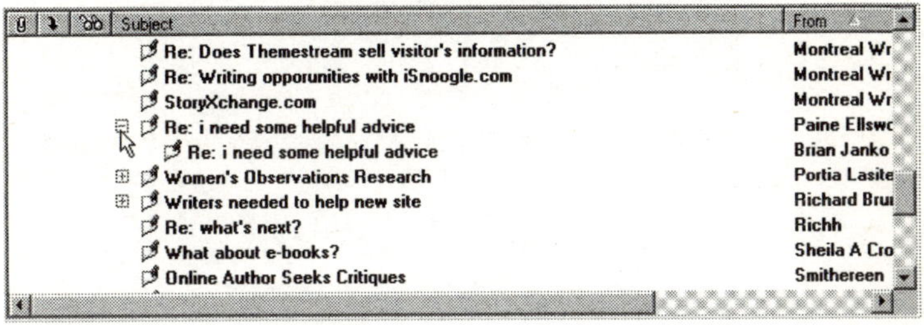

Prevent newsgroup messages from automatically downloading

1. In the **Tools** menu, click on **Options...**

2. Under the **Read** tab, clear the **Automatically downloaded message when viewing in the Preview Pane** check box.

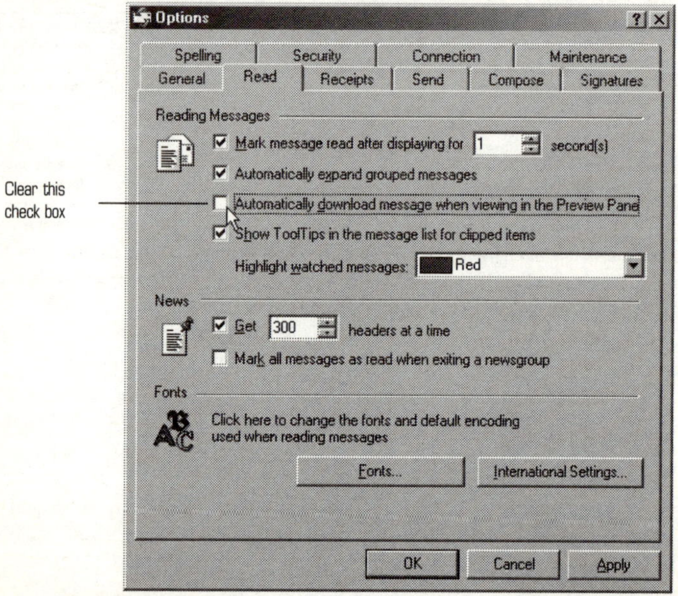

Group newsgroup messages and their replies together

1. Select a newsgroup folder.

2. In the **View** menu, point to **Current View**.

3. Click **Group Messages by Conversation**.

Conversations are grouped according to the subject title of the original message. Replies are shown as '**RE: subject title**'.

tip

To see all messages and replies, in the **Tools** menu, click on **Options...**, and under the **Read** tab, click the **Automatically expand grouped messages** check box.

Mark an individual message as read/ unread

1. Select the message.
2. In the **Edit** menu, click:

   Mark as Read

Or

   Mark as Unread.

Select as required

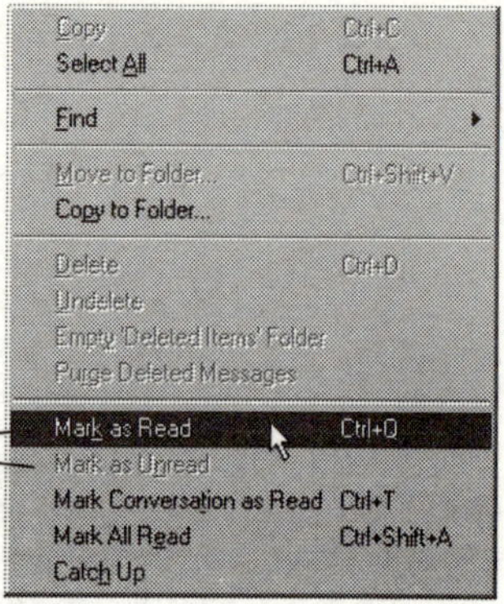

tip

To mark a selected newsgroup as read, including all messages not yet downloaded, select the newsgroup in the **Folders** list, and in the **Edit** menu click **Catch Up**.

Mark all messages as read

1. In the **Tools** menu, click on **Options…**

2. Under the **Read** tab, select the **Mark all messages as read when exiting a newsgroup** check box.

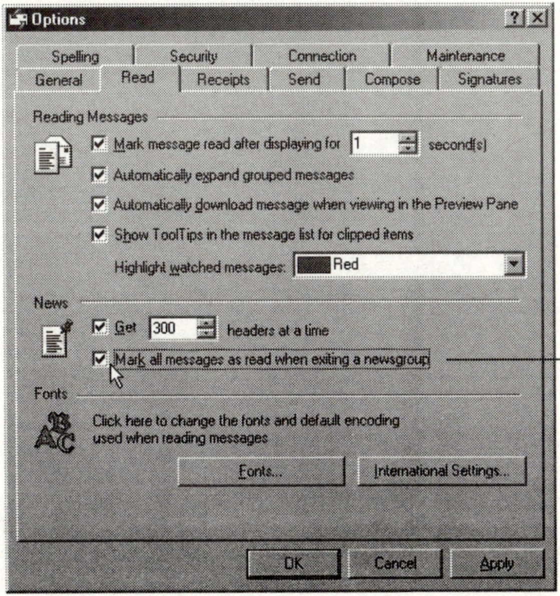

Select this option

Mark a conversation as read

1. Select either the original message or any of its replies.
2. In the **Edit** menu, click on **Mark Conversation as Read**.

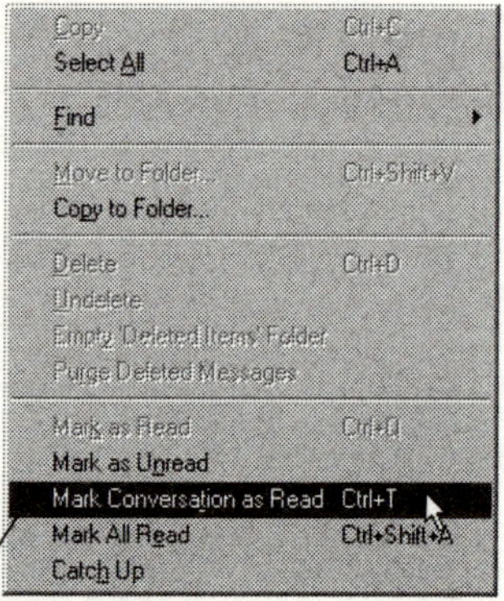

Select Mark Conversation as Read

Stop messages being automatically marked as read

1. In the **Tools** menu click on **Options…**
2. Under the **Read** tab, clear this check box:

tip

You can specify a time (in seconds) to read a message before it is marked as read in this dialog box too.

Use default views to read messages

1. In the **View** menu, point to **Current View**.
2. Click an option:

Show All Messages shows all (read and unread) messages.

Hide Read Messages shows only unread messages.

Show Downloaded Messages shows only recent downloads (IMAP and newsgroups only).

Hide Read or Ignored Messages does not show messages marked thus.

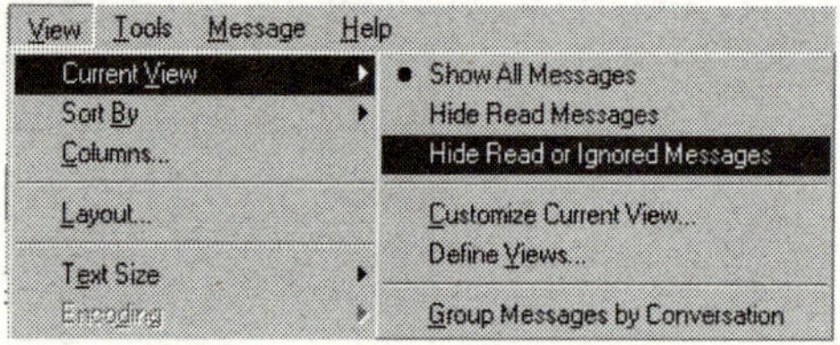

Unscramble a newsgroup message

1. In the newsgroups message list, double-click a message to open it.

2. In the **Message** menu, click **Unscramble**.

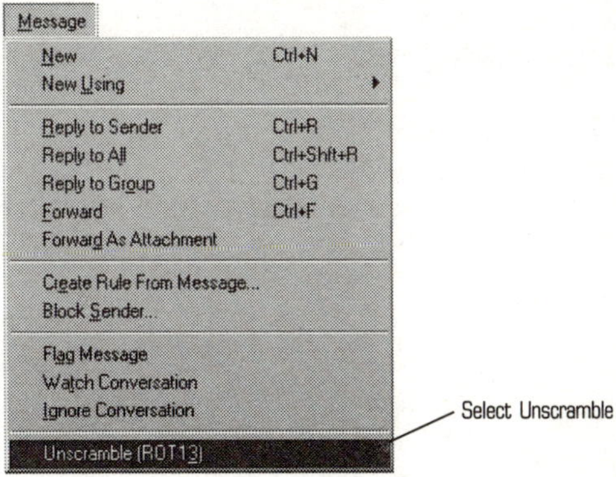

tip

This only works with incoming messages scrambled with the ROT13 method (shifting letters by 13 places). You cannot scramble outgoing messages, but you can encrypt them.

Print a message

1. Select the message.

2. Click on **Print**.

Or

Hold down **CTRL** and press **P**.

Or

In the **File** menu click on **Print…** and select the print options.

tip

You can print a message that is displayed in the preview pane or one that is open in a separate window.

Compact mail folders

1. Select a mail folder.

2. In the **File** menu, point to **Folder**.

3. Click **Compact** for the selected folder, or **Compact All Folders** for all folders.

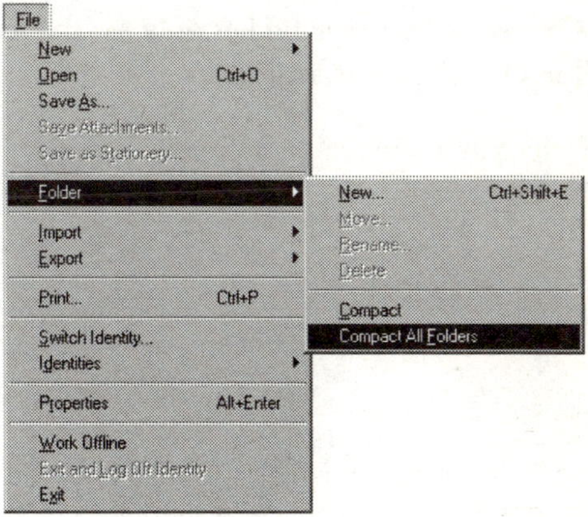

tip

Use this to save disk space after deleting messages.

Delete a news message

1. In the **Tools** menu, click on **Options…**

2. Under the **Maintenance** tab, click **Clean Up Now…**

3. Click **Browse**, and select either a news server or a single newsgroup, then click **OK**.

4. To delete message bodies only for the selected item, click the **Remove Messages** button.

5. To delete headers and messages for the selected item, click the **Delete** button.

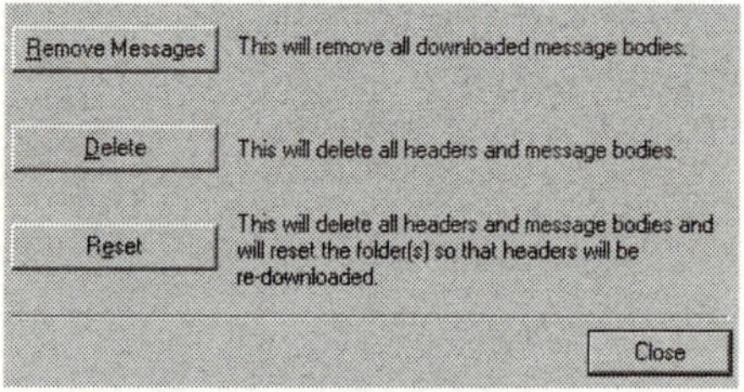

tip

News items are permanently removed from your computer, not from the news server.

Back up mail folders

Copy the folder file to a backup folder, floppy disk, or network drive using Windows Explorer.

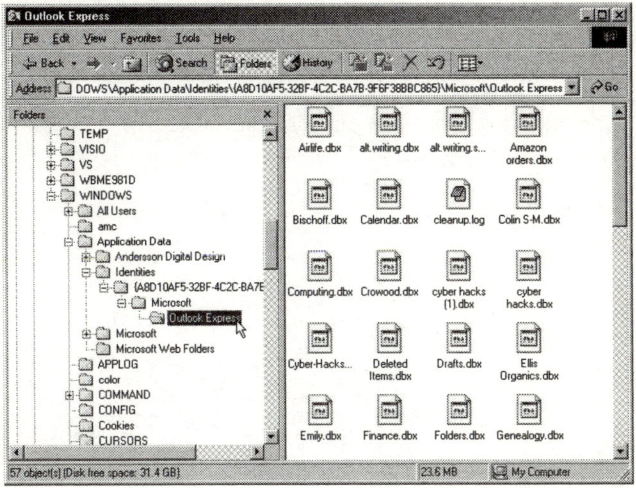

tip

Outlook Express mail folders have an .dbx extension (.mbx in Outlook Express 4).

Increase disk space by deleting stored newsgroup messages

1. In the **Tools** menu, click on **Options…**

2. Under the **Maintenance** tab, select the options required.

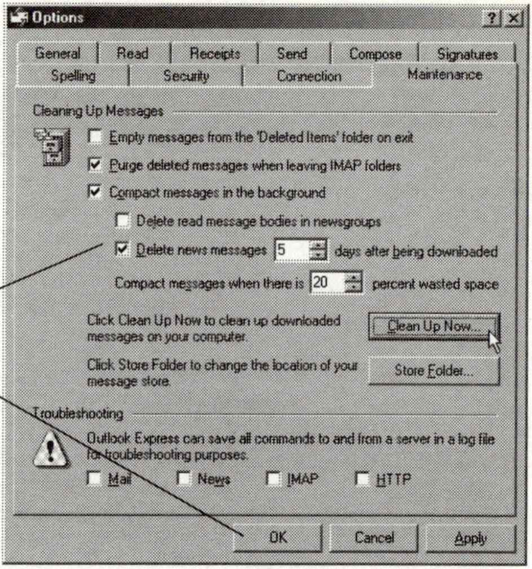

tip

To compact, delete, or remove messages from all or selected message files now, click on **Clean Up Now…**, and follow the instructions.

Remove copies of outgoing messages

1. In the **Tools** menu, click on **Options…**

2. Under the **Send** tab, clear the **Save copy of sent messages in the 'Sent Items' folder** check box.

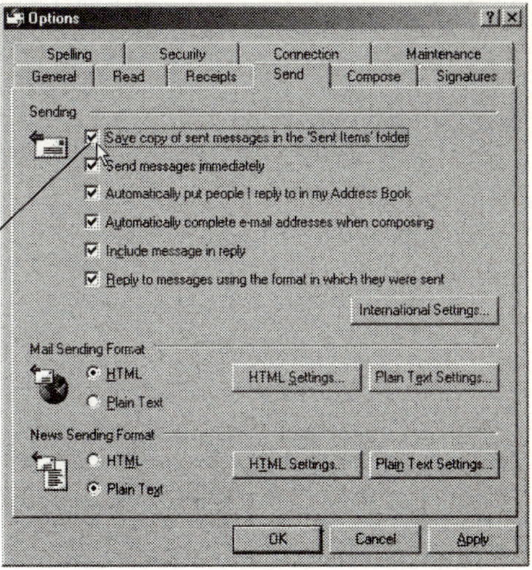

Clear this check box

tip

You can still save a copy of a message by entering your e-mail name in the **Cc:** box before sending a message.

Store messages on a mail server

1. In the **Tools** menu, click on **Accounts...**

2. Click the mail account, then click **Properties**.

3. Under the **Advanced** tab, select **Leave a copy of messages on server**.

Select Leave a copy of messages on server

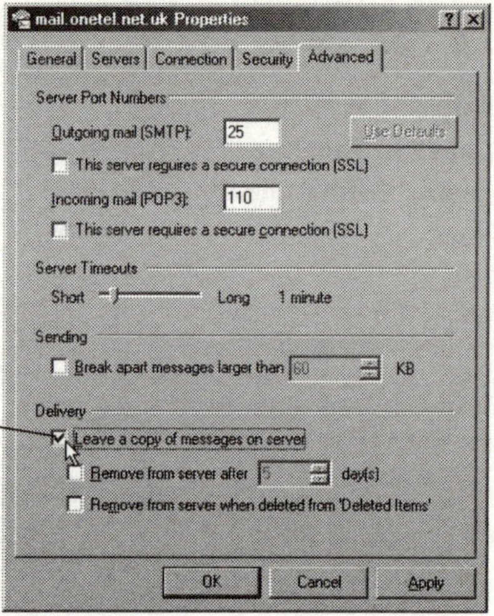

tip

This will work with POP3 and enables you to read your messages using another computer. HTTP or IMAP servers keep copies anyway.

Print a message

1. Select the message.

2. Click .

Or

2. Hold down **CTRL** and press **P**.

Or

2. In the **File** menu, click on **Print** and select the print options.

tip

You can print a message that is displayed in the preview pane or one that is open in a separate window.

Security

Sending secure messages

When sending confidential information by e-mail, it is important to be sure that documents sent are genuine and that they cannot be intercepted and read by anyone other than your intended recipient.

Outlook Express uses digital IDs to prove your identity electronically – similar to showing a driver's license. The same digital IDs can encrypt messages, keeping them private.

Set up security zones

Security zones enable you to restrict programs, such as ActiveX Controls and scripts, from running from inside HTML e-mail messages.

1. In the **Tools** menu, click on **Options...**

2. Under the **Security** tab, in the **Security Zones** section, choose an Internet Explorer security zone to use:

Internet zone (Less secure but more functional)

Restricted sites zone (More secure).

tip

Security settings made in Internet Explorer also apply to Outlook Express. See under Internet Explorer Security Zones earlier.

Digital IDs

A digital ID consists of a 'public key', a 'private key' and a 'digital signature'. Digitally signing messages adds your digital signature and public key (called a 'certificate') to the message. You may pick a certificate for others to send encrypted messages to you that is different from your signing certificate.

Recipients use your digital signature to verify your identity and can use your public key to send you encrypted mail, which you read using your private key.

To send encrypted messages, your address book must contain digital IDs for the recipients so you can use their public keys for encrypting. The recipients use their own private key to decrypt the message.

Outlook Express does all the en/decrypting for you when needed.

tip

Before sending digitally signed messages, you must obtain a digital ID. Before sending an encrypted message, you must have the recipient's digital ID in your address book.

Get a digital ID

1. In the **Help** menu click on **Contents and Index**.

2. Under the **Index** tab type '**digital ID**' into the search text box.

3. Double-click **Obtain a digital ID** and follow the instructions to connect to a Web site.

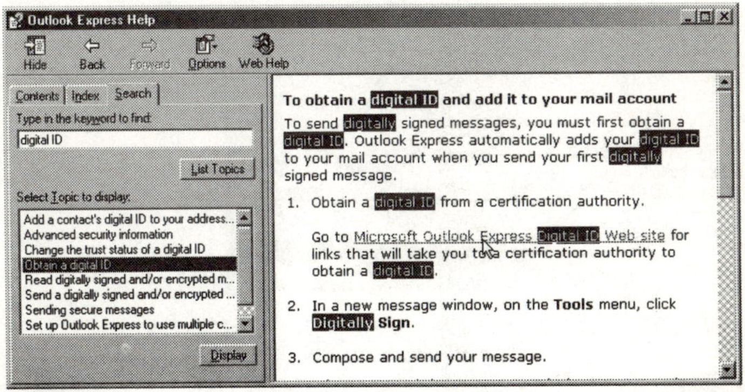

tip

See the Web site to find out more about different classes of digital ID.

Add a digital ID to your mail account

1. Obtain a digital ID as shown on the previous page.

2. In the new message window **Tools** menu, click **Digitally Sign**.

Your digital ID is automatically added to your mail account when you send your first digitally signed message.

In the Tools menu select Digitally Sign

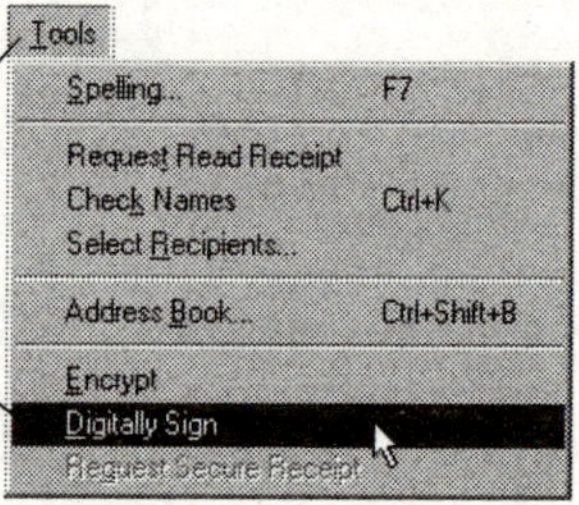

tip

With multiple mail accounts, you need a separate digital ID for each account you send secure mail from and your reply address must be in same account if you wish to receive encrypted mail.

Use multiple certificates

You may send digitally signed messages using one certificate and send encrypted messages with another. You must obtain at least one certificate before proceeding.

1. In the **Tools** menu, click on **Accounts...**

2. Select the account to use the certificate with.

3. Click on **Properties**.

4. Under the Security tab, click **Select...** for the type of certificate to use.

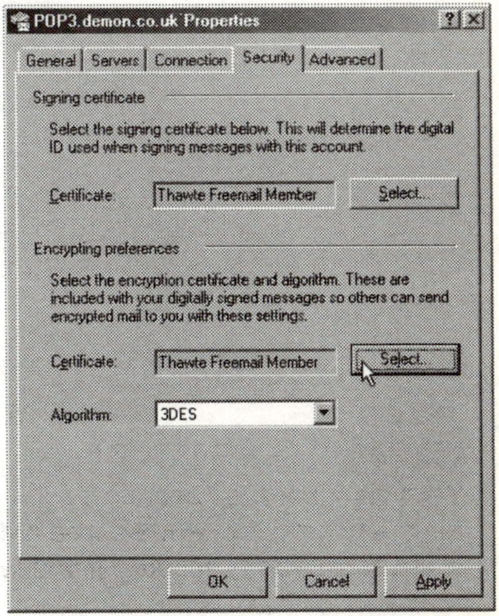

Add a contact's digital ID to your address book automatically

1. In the **Tools** menu, click on **Options...**

2. Under the **Security** tab, click **Advanced...**

3. Select the **Add senders' certificates to my address book** check box.

Select this check box

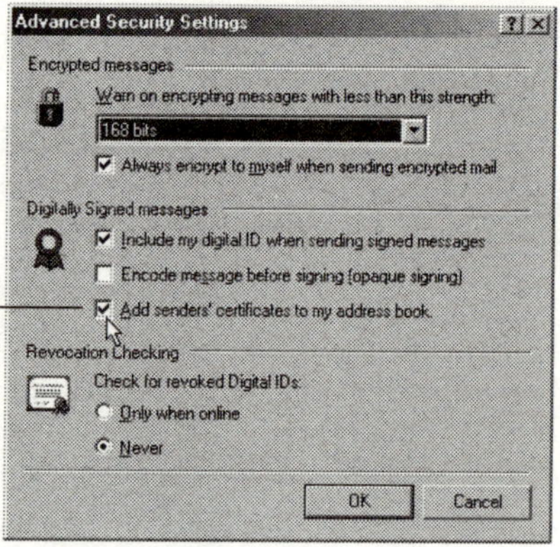

tip

When your view displays your contacts list, anyone with a digital ID in your address book will have  by their name.

Add a digital ID to your address book from another source

1. In the **Address Book**, create a new entry, or double-click an existing one.

2. Under the **Digital IDs** tab, click on **Import**.

3. Find the digital ID file, and then click **Open**.

tip

You can also get someone's digital ID by downloading it from a certification authority's Web site. Some of these are listed in the Microsoft site used in 'Getting a digital ID' above.

Change the trust status of a digital ID

The 'trust status' of a digital ID shows the degree of trust assigned to that ID. The default status in Outlook Express is 'Inherit trust from issuer'.

1. In the **Address Book**, double-click the name of the contact.

2. Under the **Digital IDs** tab select the digital ID to change, and click **Properties**.

3. Under the **Trust** tab select an option in the **Edit Trust** area.

4. Chose from:

    Inherit Trust from Issue

    Explicitly Trust this Certificate

    Explicitly Don't Trust this Certificate.

tip

The last option is better than just deleting a certificate, as you will then be warned when mail contains an untrusted certificate.

Verify a digital signature

The digital IDs of received secure messages can be checked when you open them online. A message is automatically sent to the certification authority requesting information on the digital ID used for the message.

1. In the **Tools** menu, click on **Options...**

2. Under the **Security** tab, click on **Advanced...**

3. In the **Revocation checking** section, click on **Only when online to** check digitally signed messages.

tip

You must be online to use this feature.

Send a digitally signed and/or encrypted message

In the new message window:

To digitally sign a message:

In the **Tools** menu, click **Digitally Sign**.

Or

Click on 

.

To encrypt a message:

In the **Tools** menu, click on **Encrypt**.

Or

Click on 

.

Read digitally signed and/or encrypted messages

You can read digitally signed and/or encrypted messages like any other message. The first time you open or preview a digitally signed message and/or an encrypted message a help screen will be displayed.

tip

A secure message that has doubtful security, will generate a warning before you can view the contents of the message. You can decide whether or not to view the message.

Customizing

Customize the toolbar

1. In the main window **View** menu, click **Layout…**

2. Click **Customize toolbar…**

Or

1. In the message window **View** menu, point to **Toolbars**.

2. Click **Customize…**

3. Select from the **Text Options:** list to modify the toolbar text.

4. Select from the **Icon Options:** list to modify the icon size.

5. Click the button name in the **Available toolbar buttons:** list, and then click **Add** to add a new button.

6. Click the button name in the **Current toolbar buttons:** list and then click **Remov**e to remove a button.

7. Click the button name in the **Current toolbar buttons:** list, and then click **Move Up** or **Move Down** to change button positions on the toolbar.

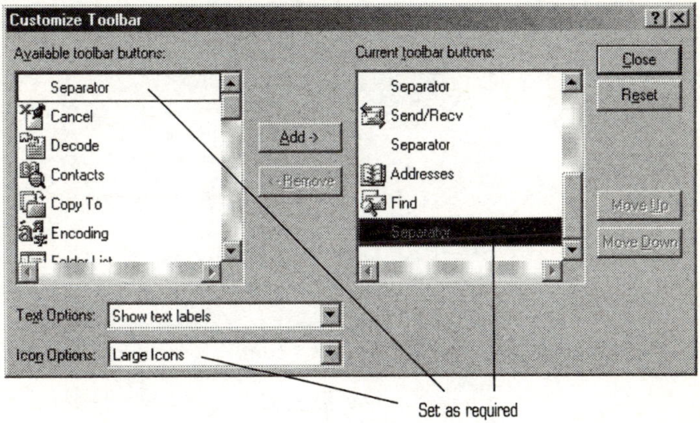

Hide or display toolbars and lists

In the **View** menu, click **Layout...**, and select your options.

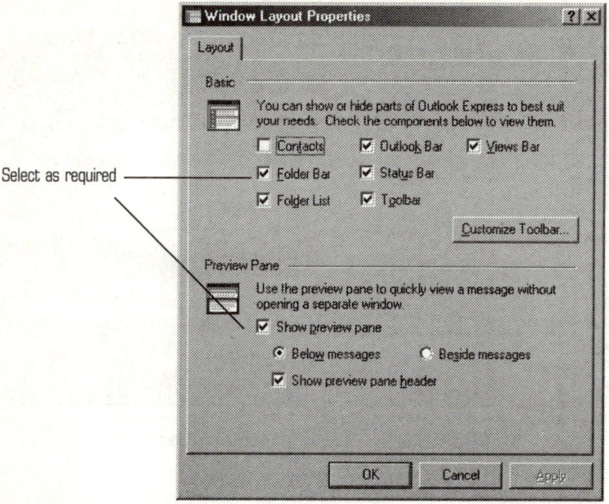

tip

To display the Outlook Express start-up window, with links to various tasks, click Outlook Express at the top of the **Folders** list.

Create and use custom views

1. In the **View** menu, point to **Current View**, then click on **Define Views…**

2. Click **New**, and in the **1. Select the Conditions for your view:** box select one or more conditions for the new view.

3. In the **2. View Description (click on an underlined value to edit it):** box click an underlined word to choose an option or to enter a value.

4. Click **Show/Hide** to show or hide messages that meet the view conditions.

5. In the **3. Name of the view:** box enter a name for the view and click **OK**.

tip

If a new view causes messages to unexpectedly disappear from view, simply change its **Show/Hide** settings.

Use the preview pane to view messages

1. In the **Tools** menu, click on **Options…**

2. Under the **Read** tab, select the **Automatically download message when viewing in the Preview Pane** check box.

Select this check box

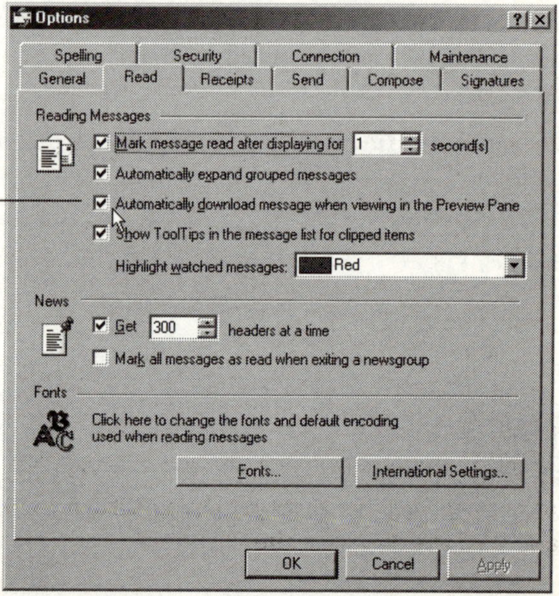

Change the display of the preview pane

The preview pane lets you view message contents without having to open another window. To preview a message, click it once. To open it in its own window, double-click it.

1. In the **View** menu, click **Layout…**
2. In the **Preview Pane** area, select your options and click **OK**.

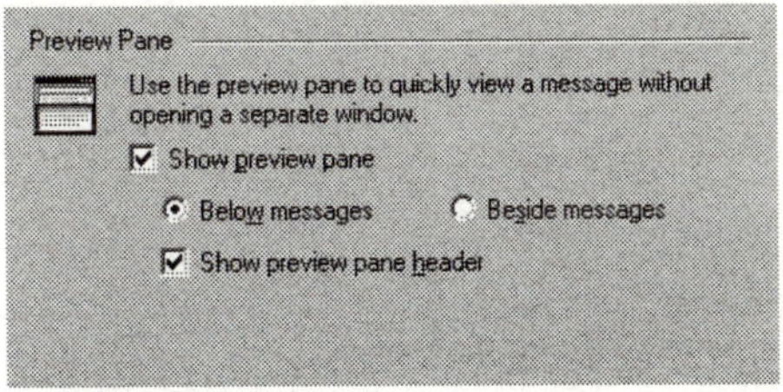

tip

To resize the preview pane and the message list, point to the divider between them until you get a double arrow or and drag the divider to size.

Change the columns displayed in the message list

1. In the **View** menu, click **Columns...**

2. To add a column, click the check box next to the column name, or select the column name and click **Show**.

3. To remove a column, clear the check box next to the column name, or select the column name and click **Hide**.

4. To change the order columns appear in, select a column name and click **Move Up** or **Move Down**.

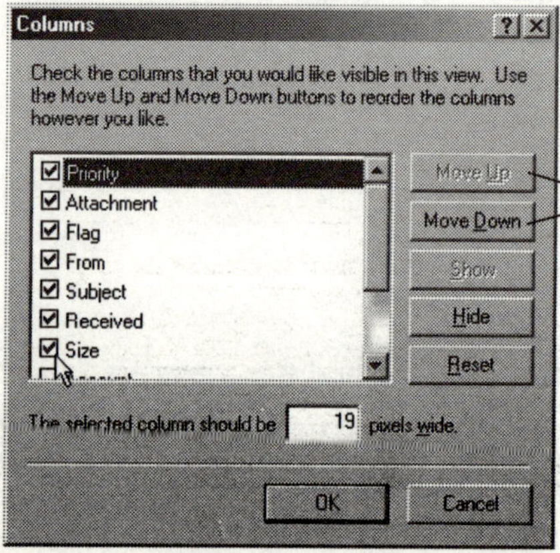

Change the order using Move Up and Move Down

Change the font used to display messages

1. In the **Tools** menu, click on **Options…**
2. Under the **Read** tab click the **Fonts…** button.
3. Change the settings as required.

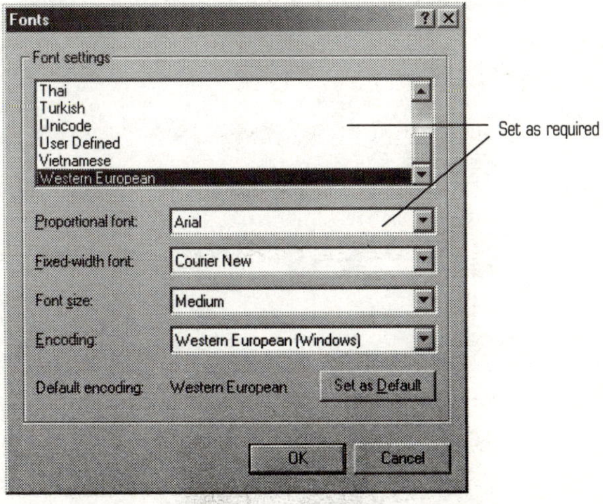

Change the text style for all messages

1. In the **Tools** menu, click on **Options…**

2. Under the **Compose** tab, click **Font Settings…**

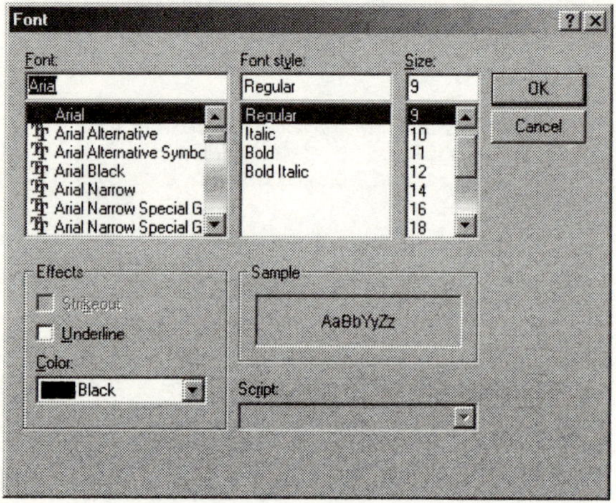

Format text within individual messages

1. In the new message window select the text to format with the mouse or in the **Edit** menu, click **Select All**.

2. On the formatting toolbar, click the buttons for the options you want.

tip

In the new message window **Format** menu ensure that a black dot appears by **Rich Text (HTML)**. With **Plain Text** selected you may have trouble formatting.

Format a paragraph

1. In the **New Messages** window, click anywhere in the paragraph, or select the text you want to format.

2. Use either the formatting toolbar or the commands in the **Format** menu to change the text.

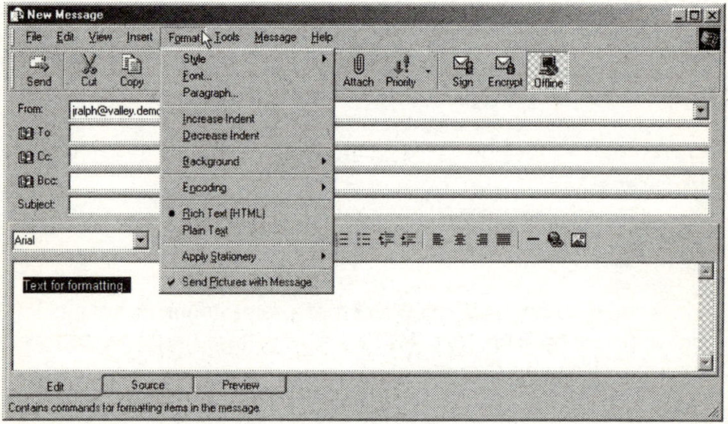

Create a numbered or bulleted list

1. In your message, click where to start the list.

2. In the **Format** menu, point to **Style**, then click either **Numbered List** or **Bulletted List**.

3. Type the first item in the list. Pressing **ENTER** starts another list entry on the next line.

4. To end the list, press **ENTER** twice.

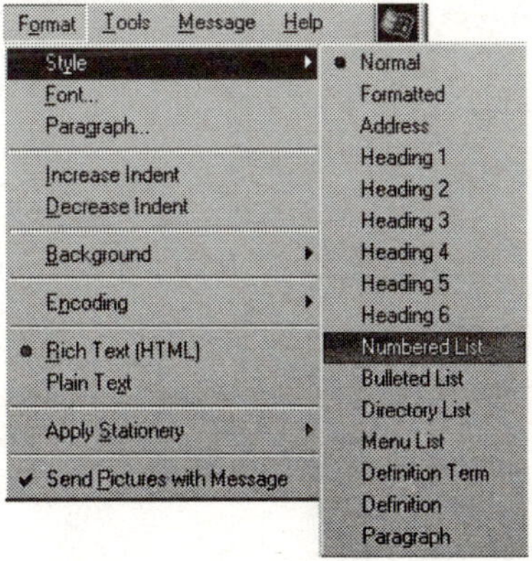

Specify what you want to download

For IMAP, HTTP, or news server folders:

1. In the **Folders** list, select an IMAP or HTTP server, or a news server.

2. In the main window, select one or more folders or newsgroups.

3. Click the **Settings...** button, and then click to change the setting to one of the following:

- **All Messages**
- **New Messages Only**
- **Headers Only**
- **Don't Synchronize** (stops downloads from that folder or newsgroup).

Receive sound notification of new messages

1. In the **Tools** menu, click on **Options…**

2. Under the **General** tab, select **Play sound when new messages arrive.**

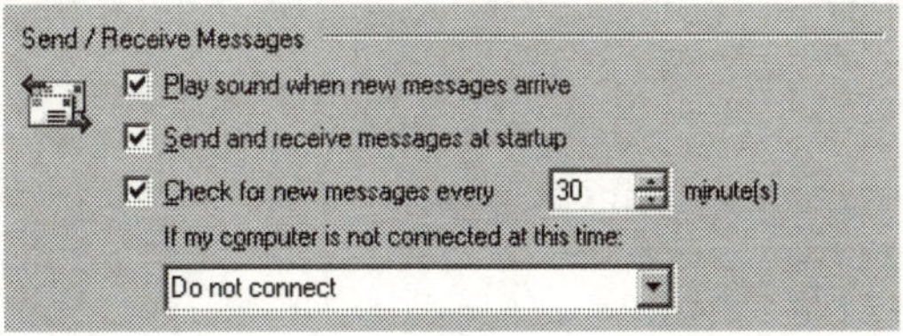

tip

The sound played can be changed through Windows. Click the Windows **Start** button and click **Settings** then **Control Panel**. Double-click on the **Sounds** icon, scroll down to and select New Mail Notification. Change the sound as required.

General

Import/Export

Export messages

1. In the **File** menu, point to **Export**, and click on **Messages**.

2. To export all the messages, click on **All folders**.

3. To export messages in one or more folders, click on **Selected folders** and then select the folders to export.

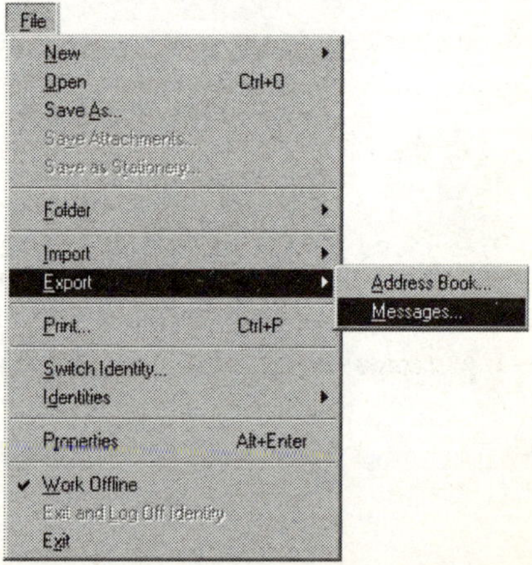

Import mail or news account settings

1. In the **File** menu, point to **Import**, and click **Mail Account Settings**

Or

News Account Settings.

2. Select the client or news account to import and click **Next.**

3. To accept the settings that appear, select **Accept settings**, click **Next** and go to step **5**.

4. To change any settings, select **Change settings**, click **Next** and follow the Wizard's instructions. When finished, click **Next.**

5. On the **Congratulations** screen, click **Finish.**

tip

In the **Tools** menu, click **Accounts** to see the account information.

Sending international messages

When you reply to a message, it is sent in the same language encoding as the original. If you change the language encoding in your reply, the original characters may not appear properly unless you are sending the message in HTML (and the receiving program can read HTML). You can also send the message using Unicode; however, not all mail and newsreading programs can display a Unicode message.

Use a different encoding for sending a single message

1. In the **Format** menu in the new message window, point to **Encoding**.

2. Click the language to use.

Set the default encoding for sending all messages

1. In the **Tools** menu, click on **Options...**

2. Under the **Send** tab, click **International Settings...**

3. Select your required default.

Flag a mail or news message

Click in the flag column in the main window, next to the message to flag.

Or

Select the message, then open the **Message** menu and click **Flag Message**.

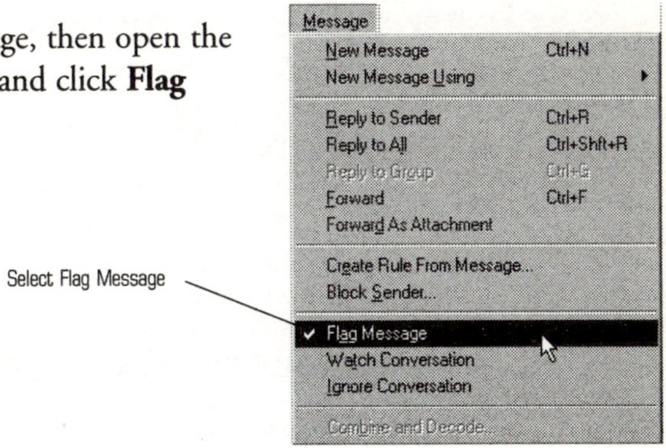

tip

Remove a flag by clicking on the flag icon beside a flagged message.

Block messages from a sender or domain

1. From your **Inbox** or a newsgroup message list, select a message from a sender to block.

2. On the **Message** menu, click **Block Sender…**

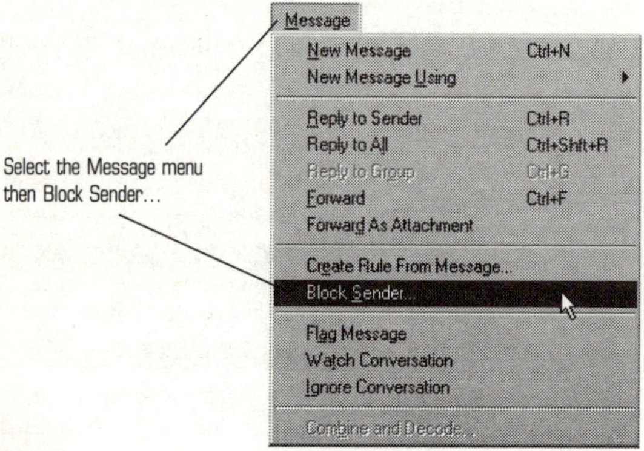

tip

This works only with POP3 mail not HTTP or IMAP messages.

Manage the blocked senders list

1. In the **Tools** menu, point to **Message Rules**, and click **Blocked Sender List…**

2. To remove an entry, select the name and click on **Remove**.

3. To change an entry, select the name and click **Modify…** Make your changes in the dialog box and click **OK**.

4. To add an entry, click **Add…** Enter the information in the dialog box and click **OK**.

5. Click **OK** in the **Message Rules** dialog box to apply rules that have been added or changed.

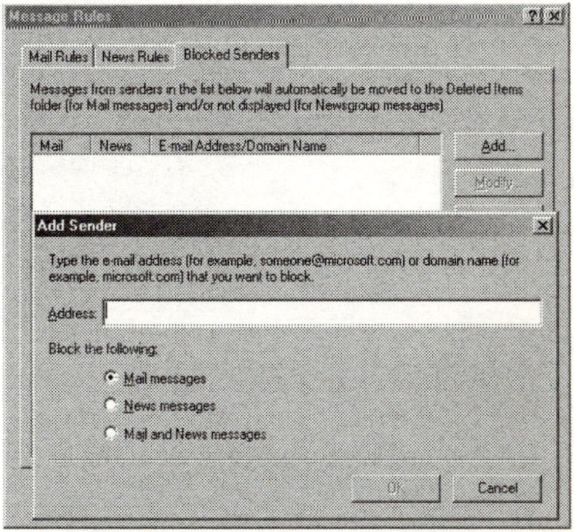

Disconnect to reduce online time automatically

1. On the **Tools** menu, click on **Options...**

2. On the **Connection** tab, select **Hang-up after sending and receiving**.

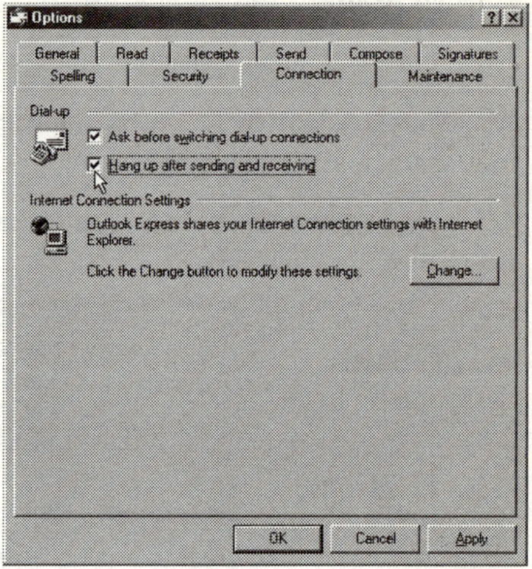

tip

Before connecting to an IMAP or HTTP server, click the server name in the folder list, and then make sure that the items you want to view offline are checked.

Reconnect to send or receive messages

1. In the **Tools** menu, point to **Send and Receive**.

Or

1. Click the drop-down arrow by the 

button.

2. Choose an option.

tip

If you select an **IMAP** folder when you are offline, and you have not checked **Work Offline** from the **File** menu, Outlook Express will reconnect, and will not hang up when you click on 

.

Change settings on an existing mail or news account

1. In the **Tools** menu, click **Accounts…**

2. Under the **Mail:** or **News:** tab, click an account, and click **Properties**.

3. Change the information as required.

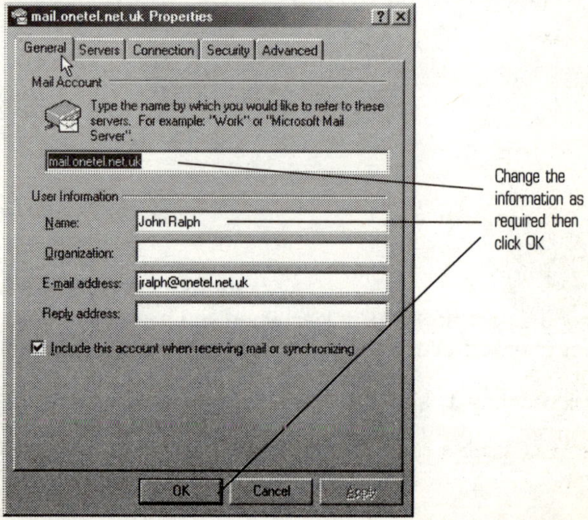

Create/delete a log file

1. In the **Tools** menu, click on **Options...**

2. Under the **Maintenance** tab, select the server to create a log for in the **Troubleshooting** section.

3. To view the log file, click the Windows **Start** icon menu, point to **Find**, and then click on **Files or Folders...**

4. In **Named:**, enter the log file name (e.g. pop3.log or imap.log).

tip

Repeat the above steps and uncheck the box in the **Troubleshooting** section when you have finished troubleshooting. Then delete the .log file in Windows Explorer if desired. Log files can take up lots of disk space.

Address Book

Open Address Book

Click 

.

Or

In the **Tools** menu select **Address Book…**

Or

Click the Windows **Start** button and click **Programs**, **Accessories** and **Address Book** successively.

Select Address Book

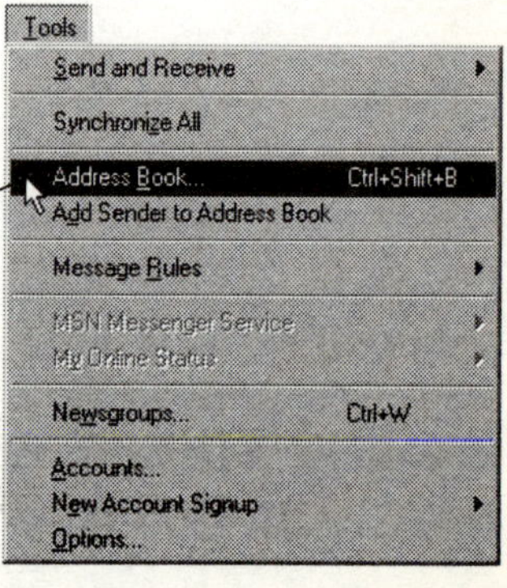

Use Address Book to address messages

1. Click the **To:**, **Cc:**, or **Bcc:** icon.

2. Select the addressee(s) from your list.

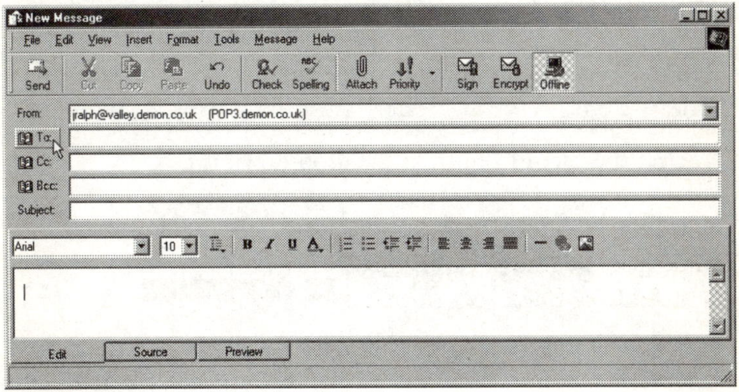

tip

Click the Windows **Start** button, point to **Find**, and then click **People...** to use the Address Book directory services directly from Windows. See page 234 for more information on directories.

Add contacts from messages

1. Select a received message.

2. In the **Tools** menu, click **Add Sender to Address Book.**

Or

1. Double-click a received message to open it.

2. In the **Tools** menu in the message window point to **Add to Address Book.**

3. Select the user to add from the drop-down list.

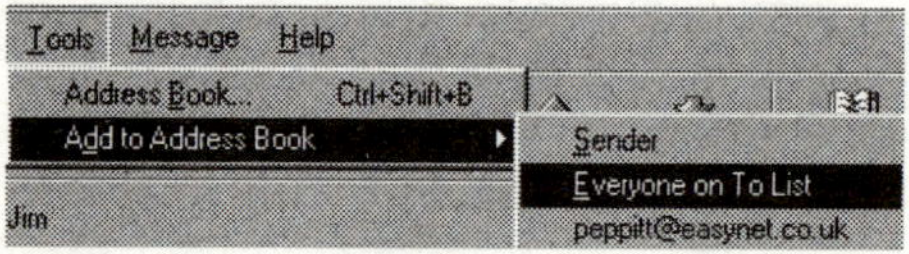

tip

The second method enables you to add some or all the recipients of the e-mail if it was sent to a group.

Add contacts to your address book automatically

1. In the **Tools** menu, click on **Options...**

2. Under the **Send** tab, click **Automatically put people I reply to in my Address Book.**

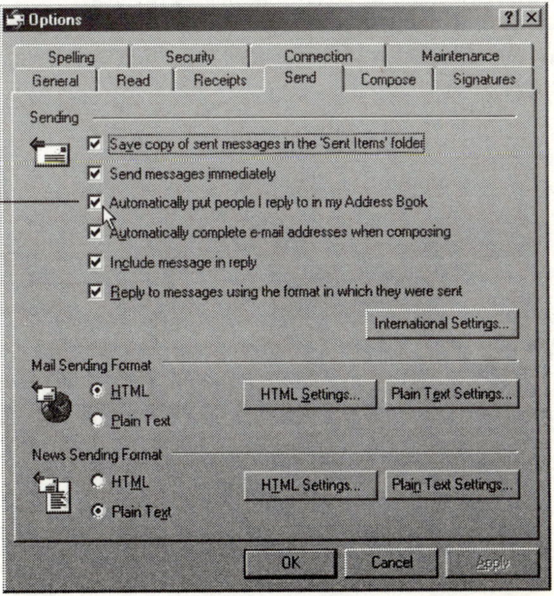

Select this check box

Add a contact manually

1. In the **Address Book**, select the folder in which to add a contact.

2. Click , then click **New Contact…**

3. Under the **Name** tab, enter at least one name for the contact. An e-mail address is useful too, for when composing messages.

4. Under the other tabs, add extra information as desired.

tip

The name displayed can be changed by typing or using the drop-down arrow beside **Display:**.

Create a group

1. In the **Address Book**, select the folder to create a group in.

2. Click 

, then click **New Group…**

3. Under the **Group** tab, in the **Group Name:** box, type the group name, then:

To add someone already in your address book, click on **Select Members**, then click their name.

To add someone new, without adding them to your address book, type their name and e-mail address in the lower half of the Properties dialog box, then click **Add…**

To add someone new to both the group and your address book, click **New Contact** and fill in the appropriate information.

4. Repeat for each member until your group is defined.

Add a contact to an existing group

1. In the **Address Book** list, double-click the required group.
2. In the group's **Properties** dialog box:

   To add someone already in your address book, click **Select Members**, then click their name.

   To add someone new, without adding them to your address book, type their name and e-mail address in the lower half of the Properties dialog box, and then click **Add...**

   To add someone new to both the group and your address book, click **New Contact...** and fill in the appropriate information.

tip

To send a message to a group of people, type the group name in the **To:** box when you send messages. Multiple groups may be created with members in more than one group.

Delete a contact from your address book

1. In the **Address book** contact list, click the contact.

2. Click .

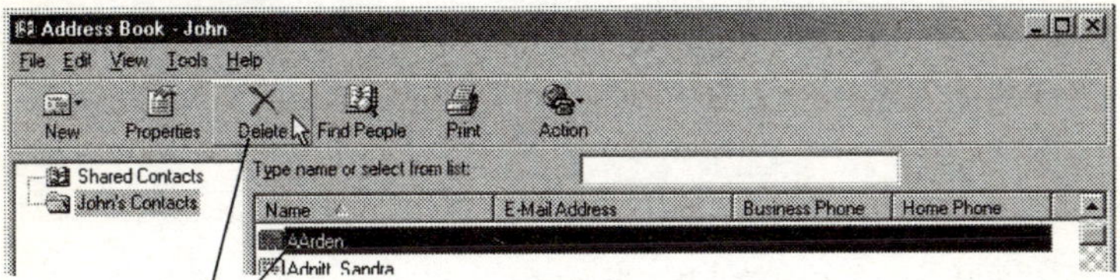

Select the contact then click Delete

tip

This also removes the contact from any groups it might be in.

Delete a contact from a group

1. In the **Address Book,** double-click the group name.

2. Under the **Group** tab, in the **Group Members:** list, click the name you want to delete.

3. Click **Remove**, then click **OK**.

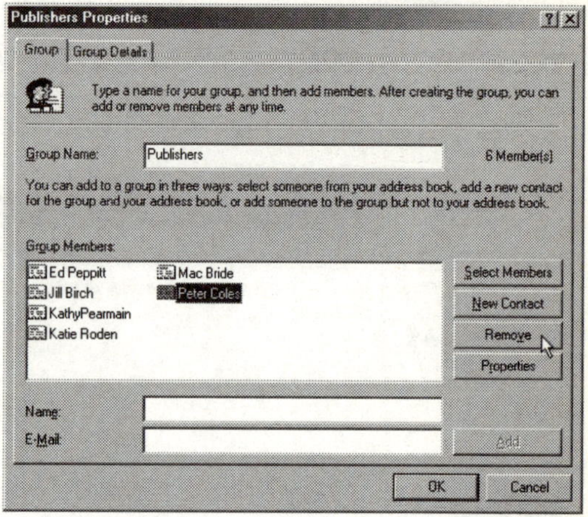

tip

The contact will remain in the address book, but not in the group.

Delete a group from the address book list

1. In the **Address Book**, click the group name.

2. Click .

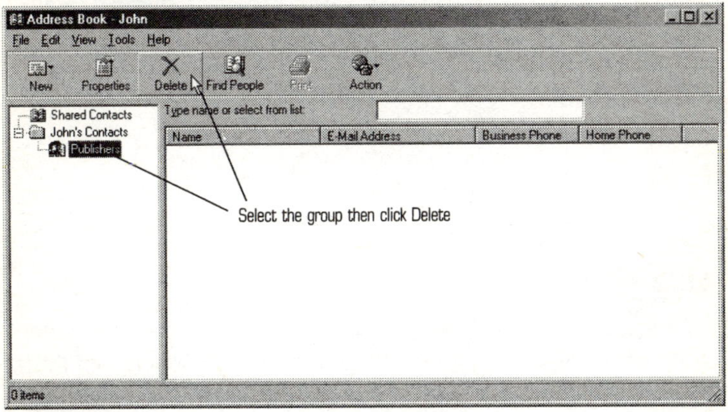

tip

The contacts will remain in your address book, but not the group.

Share a contact

1. In the **Address Book** contacts list, select the contact.

2. Drag the contact to the **Shared Contacts** folder or one of its subfolders to enable other identities to see the contact.

This removes the contact from its original folder. If you copy it across to the Shared Contacts folder by dragging using CTRL, any changes made to one copy will not be updated automatically in the other.

tip

If the Shared Contacts folder is not visible, point to the **View** menu and select **Folders and Groups**. If it is still not visible see page 225.

Identities

What are identities?

Several people may use Outlook Express and the Address Book on the same computer. Creating identities for each user means that they can each have their own address book with different contents. Different mail accounts and general Windows settings can be used as well.

Set options for identity sharing

1. In the Address Book **Tools** menu, click on **Options…**

2. Select an option.

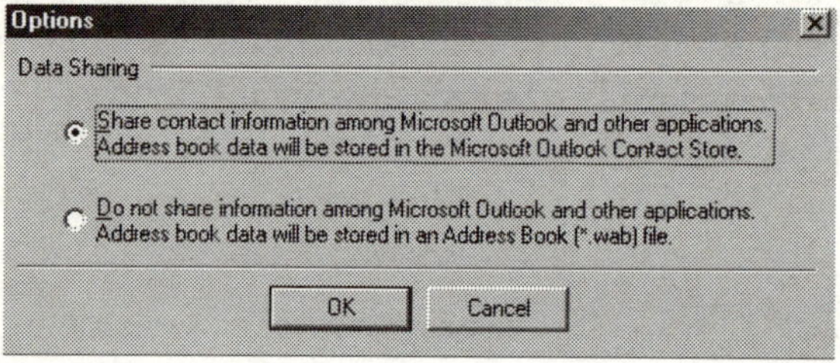

tip

The Shared Contacts folder will not be visible when only one Address Book is being used for all identities.

Add a new identity while using the Address Book

Open Address Book from Windows by clicking **Start**, **Programs**, **Accessories**, **Address Book** successively (you cannot manage identities by opening the Address Book another way).

1. In the **File** menu, click **Switch Identity…**

2. Click **Manage Identities:**

3. Click **New…**, and type the new identity name.

4. To use a password select the password requirement option and enter a password.

tip

You can add identities from Outlook Express and can also change an identity's name or password.

Delete an identity from your address book

Open Address Book from Windows by clicking **Start**, **Programs**, **Accessories**, **Address Book**.

1. In the **File** menu, click **Switch Identity…**

2. Click **Manage Identities:**

3. Select an identity, then click **Remove**.

tip

The current identity and the last remaining identity cannot be deleted.

Change the current identity's settings from the Address Book

Open Address Book from Windows by clicking **Start**, **Programs**, **Accessories**, **Address Book** .

1. In the **File** menu, click **Switch Identity…**

2. Click the **Manage Identities:** button.

3. Change any of the settings.

tip

To change an identity name or password, select it and click **Properties**.

Organize contacts and subfolders

The main folder and subfolders can hold contacts. Subfolders are always in alphabetical order and cannot be reorganized. A new identity folder is automatically created when a new identity is created.

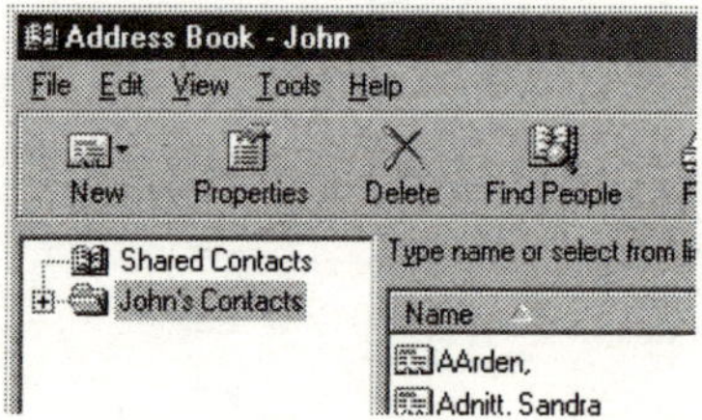

tip

If you cannot see the folders on the left, point to the **View** menu and select **Folders and Groups**.

Create a subfolder

1. Select the folder to put the subfolder in.
2. Click .

3. Click **New Folder…**
4. Type the new name and click **OK**.

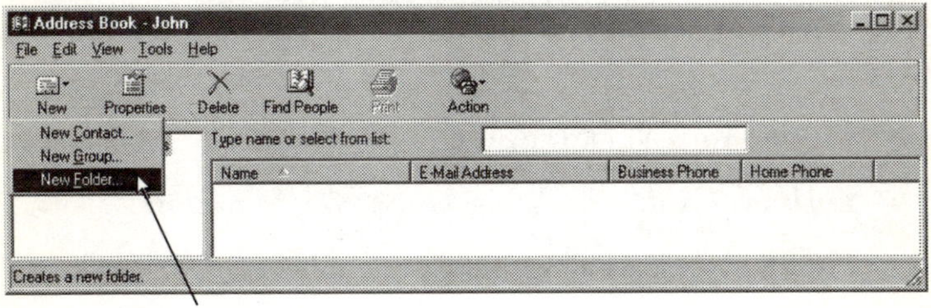

Click New Folder…

tip

The Main Identity's Contacts and the Shared Contacts folders cannot be deleted.

Print contacts

1. In the **Address Book**, select the contact(s) to print.

2. Click on **Print**.

3. In the **Print Range** area of the Print dialog box, select:

    All to print all contacts

    Selection to print your selection.

4. In the **Print Style** area of the Print dialog box, select a printing style:

    Memo prints all information

    Business Card prints business-related information

    Phone List prints a list of phone numbers.

tip

In the Print dialog box click the **Properties** button to customize output depending on your printer.

Import an address book from another program

From other Windows Address Book files (WAB):

1. In the Address Book **File** menu, point to **Import**, and click **Address Book (WAB)...**

2. Find the Address Book to import, and click **Open**.

For Netscape Communicator, Microsoft Exchange Personal Address Book, or any text (CSV) file:

1. In the Address Book **File** menu, point to **Import**, then click **Other Address Book...**

2. Click the address book or file type to import, then click **Import**.

tip

If your address book type is not listed, export it to a text (CSV) file or an LDIF (LDAP Directory Interchange Format) file, and import it as that type.

Export your address book contacts to other programs

To another Windows Address Book:

1. In the Address Book **File** menu, point to **Export**, and click **Address Book (WAB)…**

2. Find the Windows Address Book file you want to export to, and then click **Open**.

For all other address book formats:

1. In the Address Book **File** menu, point to **Export**, and click **Other Address Books…**

2. Click the address book or file type to export to, and click **Export**.

tip

Export and import will not work if Data Sharing is enabled. See page 225.

What are directory services?

A directory service is a search engine you can use to find people and businesses on the Internet. Address Book has several directory services built-in and you can also add additional ones.

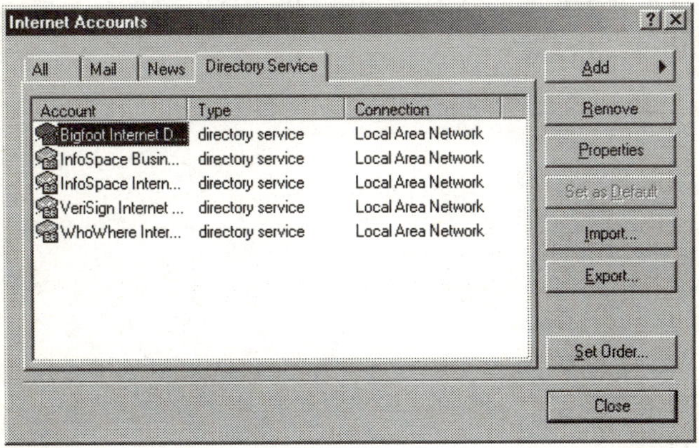

tip

If a search fails with one directory, try others.

Find people on the Internet

1. Click 

on the **Address Book** toolbar.

2. Select the directory from the **Look in:** drop-down list.

3. Under the **People** tab, type the name or e-mail address of the person to search for.

4. Click **Find Now**.

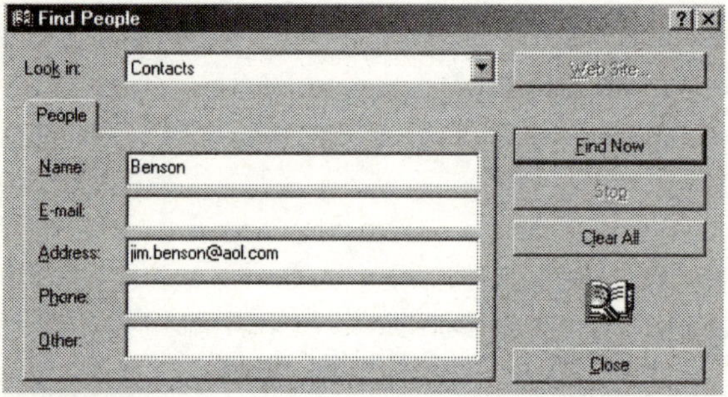

Refine search criteria

4. Carry out steps **1** to **3** above. Then under the **Advanced** tab, using the drop-down lists in the first two boxes as necessary, define your criteria in the three boxes, and then click **Add...**

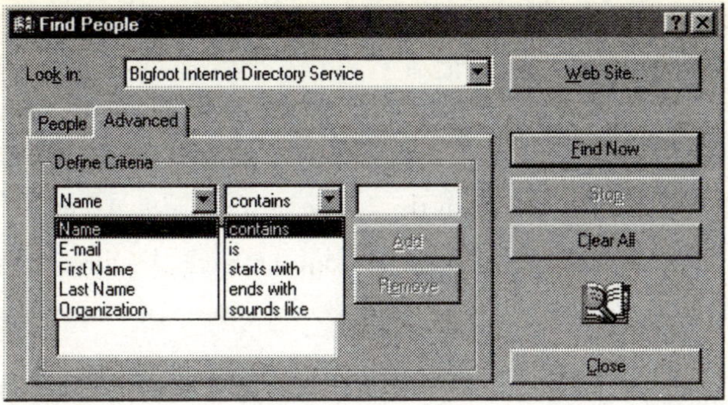

5. Repeat until all your criteria are entered (if you make a mistake, select the item in the **Define criteria** list box and click **Remove**).

tip

Using **starts with** or **is** will make for a faster search. Use **contains**, **ends with**, or **sounds like** if initial searches fail.

Change search settings for a directory service

1. In the **Tools** menu in either Address Book or Outlook Express, click **Accounts...**

2. On the **Directory Service** tab double-click the directory service.

3. On the **Advanced** tab, in the **Search** area, change the settings as required.

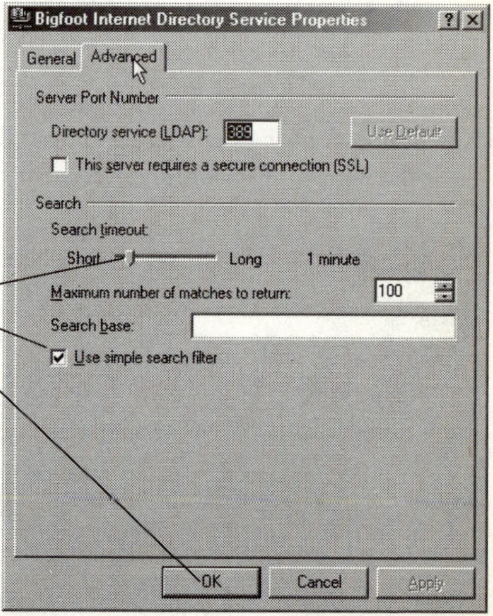

Change the settings as required then click OK

Set up a directory service to check for e-mail addresses

1. In the **Tools** menu in Address Book or Outlook Express, click on **Accounts…**

2. Under the **Directory Service** tab select a directory service.

3. Click **Properties**.

4. Under the **General** tab, select the **Check name against this server when serving mail** check box.

tip

If you cannot remember someone's complete e-mail address you can now type a partial name in the Outlook Express new message address box then, in the **Tools** menu, click **Check Names**. Outlook Express will first check your address book for the name and then the directory service.

Change the order in which directory services are checked

1. In the **Tools** menu in Address Book or Outlook Express, click on **Accounts…**

2. Under the **Directory Service** tab click **Set Order…**

3. Select a directory service, then click **Move Up** or **Move Down**.

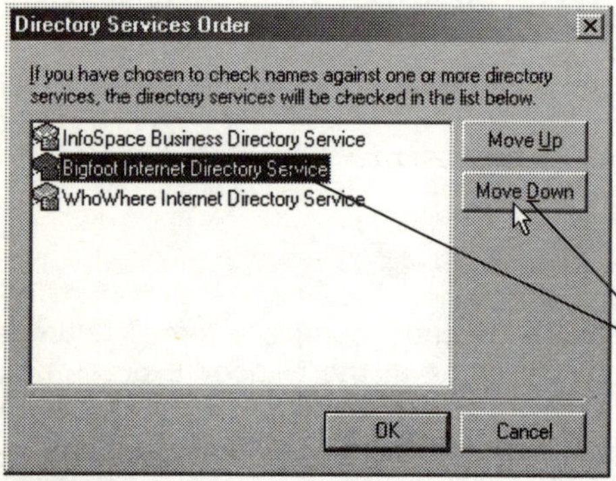

Select the directory then click Move Up or Move Down

tip

You must set up directory services to check for addresses first. See page 238.

Add a directory service

First obtain the server name from the directory service provider.

1. In the **Tools** menu in Address Book or Outlook Express, click on **Accounts…**

2. If in Outlook Express, under the **Directory Service** tab, click **Add…**, then click **Directory Service…**

Or

If in the Address Book, just click **Add…**

3. Follow the instructions in the **Internet Directory Server Name Wizard**.

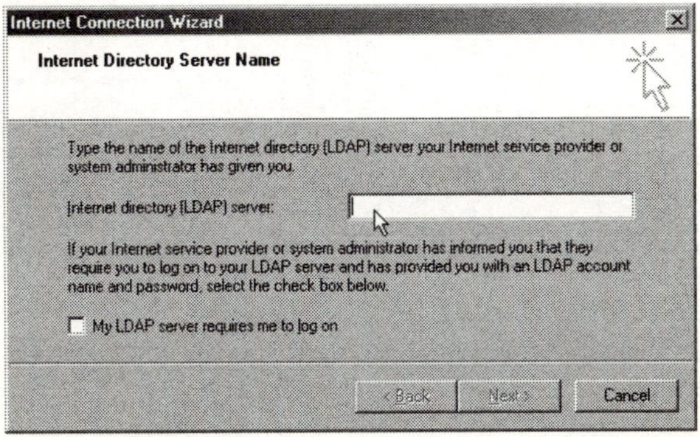

Delete a directory service

1. In the **Tools** menu in Address Book or Outlook Express, click on **Accounts…**

2. Under the **Directory Service** tab select the directory service.

3. Click **Remove**.

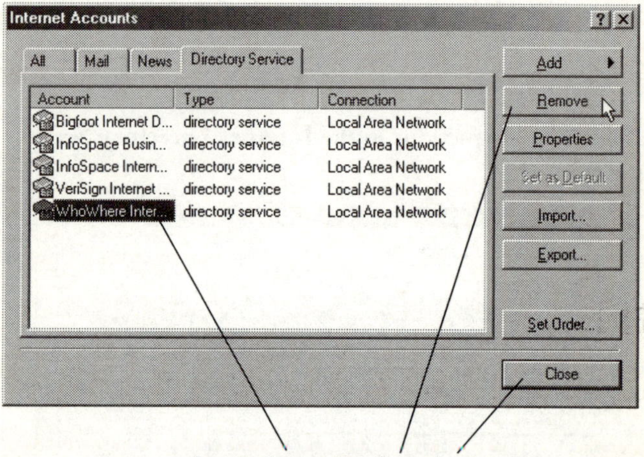

Select the directory, click on Remove then Close

Create a business card

A business card is Address Book information about you, stored in a widely used format. Your contact information must be in your address book before you can create one.

1. Select your name from the Address Book list.

2. In the **File** menu, point to **Export**, then click **Business Card (vCard)...**

3. Select a location in which to store the file, then click **Save**.

tip

To add your business card to a message, in the **Insert** menu, click **My Business Card**.

Import a business card

1. In the Address Book **File** menu, point to **Import**, then click **Business Card (vCard)…**

2. Locate the business card file on your computer or a network drive, select it, then click **Open**.

3. Alter the contact information in the dialog box as required.

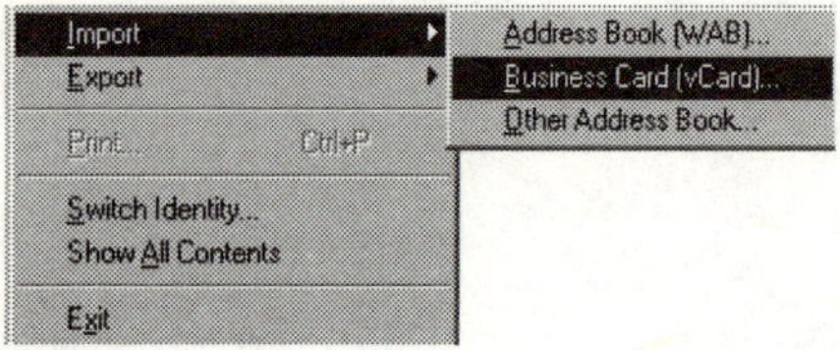

tip

You cannot import if Data Sharing is enabled. See page 225.